THE

Husband

SHE WANTS

**12 SECRETS
TO BECOMING
A DESIRABLE
MAN OF GOD**

ELANGE NATHAN

THE

Husband

SHE WANTS

**12 SECRETS
TO BECOMING
A DESIRABLE
MAN OF GOD**

DR. ELANGE NATHAN

Copyright Notice

The Husband She Wants
12 Secrets to Becoming a Desirable Man of God

Published by Anointed Fire House
Cover Design by Anointed Fire
www.anointedfirehouse.com

ISBN-13: 978-1-7331127-5-8

I have tried to recreate events, locales and conversations from my memories of them. In order to maintain their anonymity in some instances I have changed the names of individuals and places, I may have changed some identifying characteristics and details such as physical properties, occupations and places of residence.

TABLE OF CONTENTS

Introduction

A man cannot be a husband unless he first
understands sonship. God created you and
gave you authority over all. Then, He created
the woman. You called her "flesh of my flesh."
Adam understood his place and the purpose of
creation. Before a man can enter a relationship
with a woman, he has to first understand and
establish a relationship with his Creator.

He created and chose you.
*Ye have not chosen me, but I have chosen
you, and ordained you, that ye should go and
bring forth fruit, and that your fruit should
remain.*
John 15:16

**He called you to be a son, servant, and a
friend.**
When God calls you, the devil retaliates. If you
are fighting a great battle today, it's because
God has called you to greatness. All of these
tribulations that the enemy has sent your way

are designed to stop you. What does the devil know about your destiny that you don't? What level of threat does your ministry, marriage and your children present to Satan's kingdom? He's obviously scared of you and that's why he attacks you. In this book, I will unveil the twelve secrets to win every attack against your destiny and become the well-sought after man, according to the will of God for your destiny.

CHAPTER 1

The Three Dimensions of a Relationship with God

Sonship

Being a **son of God** is a conscious decision; this decision requires you to accept Jesus Christ as your Lord and Savior and follow Him and Him only. John 1:12 says, "*But as many as received him, to them gave he power to become the sons of God, even to them that believe on his name.*" Man was not created to be like the animal; man was created for relationship. A man without God is no man at all. You belong to God. Though many have tried to go on without Him, they have soon come to realize that a life without God is full of voids. When you become a son of God, you become totally dependent on Him. Your life then becomes like that of a child; you become His student. God will then put in an appointed place with the people He has assigned to grow and nurture you. They will help you to **develop** in your relationship with Him and with the body of Christ; they will help to **mature** you in understanding and wisdom, and they will help to **increase** you in unity of faith, stature, and fullness of Christ.

And he gave some, apostles; and some, prophets; and some, evangelists; and some, pastors and teachers; For the perfecting of the saints, for the work of the ministry, for the edifying of the body of Christ: Till we all come in the unity of the faith, and of the knowledge of the Son of God, unto a perfect man, unto the measure of the stature of the fullness of Christ. Ephesians 4:11-14

Grow = Develop + Mature + Increase

Servanthood

Though many have their own definitions of servanthood, it's best to understand it through theological psychology. Through years of research, Dr. J. Arno at the National Christian

Counselors Association has developed *The "Supine" Temperament* which is now known by Christian and secular counseling scholars as the fifth temperament. A supine is a natural-born, faithful servant. It is an inborn temperament gifted by God to only a select few. A servant is a minister—one who is serving from the heart, by faith, to advance God's kingdom. A supine doesn't serve for money. Though their only desired reward is a faithful relationship, God rewards them with substance. In God's Kingdom, promotion and titles only come through servanthood.

Now faith is the substance of things hoped for, the evidence of things not seen.
Hebrews 11:1

Even so faith, if it hath not works, is dead being alone.
James 2:17

This scripture clarifies it all. A man who is serving is a man who is waiting for the answers to his prayers from the Lord. **When you are**

waiting on a table at a restaurant, you are serving that table. If you are doing the same thing at your church, you are a servant or, better yet, a minister of the gospel.

But they that wait upon the Lord shall renew their strength; they shall mount up with wings as eagles; they shall run, and not be weary; and they shall walk, and not faint.
Isaiah 40:31

The verb "wait" in this scripture means to "serve"; such as, a waiter or a server at a restaurant. Our waiting on the Lord is not to stand by idly, but to work (serve). When you speak to God, He speaks back to you. A servant has an intimate relationship with the Lord through prayer and servanthood. A man who is serving has positioned himself to engage his ears where he can hear God. A complete life cannot be fulfilled without service to others.

Then the princes of the Philistines went forth: and it came to pass, after they went forth, that

The Three Dimensions of a Relationship with God

David behaved himself more wisely than all the servants of Saul; so that his name was much set by.
1 Samuel 18:30

The servants of God are the most dangerous people for anyone to criticize, attack, or ridicule. The best thing one can do for a servant is to serve them as they serve.

And of the angels he saith, Who maketh his angels spirits, and his ministers a flame of fire.
Hebrews 1:7

Saying, Touch not mine anointed, and do my prophets no harm.
1 Chronicles 16:22

A man's greatest weapon against his enemies is his anointing. This weapon will break him free from all kinds of demonic powers and stand in the gap for him, his family and even his friends.

And it shall come to pass in that day, that his

burden shall be taken away from off thy shoulder, and his yoke from off thy neck, and the yoke shall be destroyed because of the anointing.
Isaiah 10:27

Servant = Faith + Attitude

Six Steps to Servanthood

1) **Relationship -** The first biggest decision a man will ever make in his life is when he gives his life back to Jesus Christ, accepts Him as his Lord and Savior and then commences to follow Him. The biggest accomplishment of a servant of God is when he recognizes and becomes familiar with the voice of God. *My sheep hear my voice, and I know them, and they follow me: John 10:27.*

2) **Fellowship –** in the beginning of 2016, there was a great coming back to the church. Congregations across the world have seen an increase in attendance.

This means that there is a greater need for the church body to walk in unity so that the mentoring and training processes can take place. We need to position ourselves to counsel, teach, and feed God's people; consequentially, sons will become servants and will give birth to more sons and daughters for the kingdom of God. Since the year 2000, governments have been looking to the church for humanitarian, immigration, and spiritual leadership. Your salvation comes from God, but your church needs you so they can come together in unity, faith, and body. *Not forsaking the assembling of ourselves together, as the manner of some is; but exhorting one another: and so much the more, as ye see the day approaching (Hebrew 10:25).*

The Six (6) Disciplines of Fellowship

Spiritual Growth: When you remain in the discipline of fellowship, you will experience extraordinary Spiritual Growth through the blessing of covenant relationships, corporate prayer, worship and community.

And they continued steadfastly in the apostles' doctrine and fellowship, and in breaking of bread, and in prayers.
Act 2:42

Love: The greatest test is the test of love. A man who has remained in the discipline of love is one who has surrendered himself to the trial of love. When you are in the fellowship of love, you will experience offense by your community. God uses the church to prepare us for marriage and family. Fellowship teaches us to focus on the love that we have for one another, instead of one another's shortcomings; fellowship teaches and encourages us to pray for each other. You will succeed greatly in your relationship with your wife and children if you have mastered the ability to focus on love instead of offense.

No man hath seen God at any time. If we love

one another, God dwelleth in us, and his love
is perfected in us.
1 John 4:12

Encourage: When a man sins, he experiences shame and guilt. These are the weapons the enemy uses to discourage him out of fellowship with the brethren and eventually with God. This is why community is vital to a man's survival. All men have varying weaknesses, but together, we are all strong.

But exhort one another daily, while it is called
Today; lest any of you be hardened through
the deceitfulness of sin.
Hebrew 3:13

Serve: When you are serving with each other, don't forget to serve one another. It is easier to humble yourself with people who operate in love than people who operate in selfishness. Whatever you will need in life will come through serving. Every anointing God has poured unto a man's life was for service. You must position yourself to receive.

For, brethren, ye have been called unto liberty;
only use not liberty for an occasion to the flesh,
but by love serve one another.
Galatians 5:13

Honor: God is calling you to be loyal, faithful, and to receive your brethren as Christ has received you. Honoring is one of the most difficult tasks for men; this is because they are so busy seeking honor that they almost have no time to honor one another. As we honor God, we can use this opportunity to grow, build and display a godly fellowship with the brethren.

Be kindly affectioned one to another with
brotherly love; in honor preferring one another.
Romans 12:10

Compassion: When you have compassion, you will display a forgiving and none accusatory approach. Your compassion for community is the number one way to show the love of God to others.

And be ye kind one to another, tenderhearted, forgiving one another, even as God for Christ's sake hath forgiven you.
Ephesians 4:32

3) **Followership**: Jesus said to the disciples to follow Him. According to Merriam Webster, the verb "to follow" means to come into experience. Followership speaks to your capacity or willingness to follow a leader. The disciples of Jesus followed Him as a student follows a teacher. The root word of discipline is disciple. It comes from the Latin word "discipulus", which means pupil or student. The men who submitted themselves to be disciplined by Christ eventually grew to become teachers also.

And he said to them all, If any man will come after me, let him deny himself, and take up his cross daily, and follow me.
Luke 9:23

11

And he saith unto them, Follow me, and I will make you fishers of men.
Matthew 4:19

And the things that thou hast heard of me among many witnesses, the same commit thou to faithful men, who shall be able to teach others also.
2 Timothy 2:2

4) **Partnership:** From the very beginning of time, God created the heavens and the earth, and He put man on earth to cultivate it. God created everything, and whatsoever man called it, so it was. Though this relationship between man and God was destroyed by sin, Jesus came to reestablish this partnership. Those He called to be His disciples, He also equipped and sent out.

Go ye therefore, and teach all nations, baptizing them in the name of the Father, and of the Son, and of the Holy Ghost.

Matthew 28:19

But made himself of no reputation, and took upon him the form of a servant, and was made in the likeness of men.
Philippians 2:7

5) **Stewardship:** Your partnership with God begins when you become a good manager of God's gift in your life. God gives gifts; your job is to manage those gifts according to your assignment and the calling of God in your life. A great servant makes a great steward.

You have been faithful with few things, I will make you ruler of many things.
James 1:25

In the following scriptures, Jesus explained the importance of being a good steward. God is the giver and men are caretakers. When you manage God's money and wealth, He rewards you with more. Jesus said:
For the kingdom of heaven is as a man

traveling into a far country, who called his own servants, and delivered unto them his goods. And unto one he gave five talents, to another two, and to another one; to every man according to his several ability; and straightway took his journey. Then he that had received the five talents went and traded with the same, and made them other five talents. And likewise he that had received two, he also gained other two. But he that had received one went and digged in the earth, and hid his lord's money. Matthew 25:14-18

God is not going to come down from heaven to manage the bank, restaurant and the real estate company He gave you. He is not going to embark on a mission trip to Africa or engage in the finances of your church because He has created you with all the wisdom necessary to accomplish your assignment. So, He gave you substance for the advancement of His kingdom on earth.

After a long time the lord of those servants cometh, and reckoneth with them. And so he

that had received five talents came and brought other five talents, saying, Lord, thou deliveredst unto me five talents: behold, I have gained beside them five talents more. His lord said unto him, well done, thou good and faithful servant: thou hast been faithful over a few things, I will make thee ruler over many things: enter thou into the joy of thy lord. He also that had received two talents came and said, Lord, thou deliveredst unto me two talents: behold, I have gained two other talents beside them. His lord said unto him, Well done, good and faithful servant; thou hast been faithful over a few things, I will make thee ruler over many things: enter thou into the joy of thy lord.
Matthew 25:19-23

A good steward manages what God has given to him, and he manages it all well. So, go ahead, cultivate and grow because on that set day, God will ask for an account of everything He has given you. Have you fed the hungry, clothed the poor and sheltered the homeless? God will not come down or send an angel to do for you anything He has already equipped you to do for yourself or your brethren.

Then he which had received the one talent came and said, Lord, I knew thee that thou art an hard man, reaping where thou hast not sown, and gathering where thou hast not strawed: And I was afraid, and went and hid thy talent in the earth: lo, there thou hast that is thine. His lord answered and said unto him, Thou wicked and slothful servant, thou knewest that I reap where I sowed not, and gather where I have not strawed: Thou oughtest therefore to have put my money to the exchangers, and then at my coming I should have received mine own with usury. Take therefore the talent from him, and give it unto him which hath ten talents. For unto every one that hath shall be given, and he shall have abundance: but from him that hath not shall be taken away even that which he hath. And cast ye the unprofitable servant into outer darkness: there shall be weeping and gnashing of teeth". Matthew 25:24-30

God is the only one who gives and He gives freely

But who am I, and what is my people, that we should be able to offer so willingly after this sort? For all things come of thee, and of thine own have we given thee.
1 Chronicles 29.14

6) **Worship:** Worship is the protocol to God's presence. When a man humbles himself before his Creator, the hand of God will move in his favor. This stage of our relationship is about God and your attitude.

But the hour cometh, and now is, when the true worshippers shall worship the Father in spirit and in truth: for the Father seeketh such to worship him.
John 4:23

Thou wilt shew me the path of life: in thy presence is fulness of joy; at thy right hand there are pleasures for evermore.
Psalm 16:11

Friendship

Friendships are more special than any other types of relationships. It is defined by time spent together, communication, loyalty, and reciprocity. Just like a natural relationship, when you become a friend of God, He speaks with you. This level of relationship is an intimate one. Sons and servants who operate in the realm of the prophetic are known as friends of God.

Friends have a covenant connotation. Jonathan and David made a mutual covenant between them; Abraham was a covenant friend of God. What does this mean? Loyalty, provision, protection, and sacrificial love— these were not qualities that were always found in brothers by birth. It should come as no surprise that Jesus, during His last meeting with His disciples, declared them to be His "friends" *(John 15:13-15).* He then demonstrated the most telling trait of true friendship: the willingness to lay down one's life for another. All who walk in covenant with

Jesus Christ are assured of His loyalty, provision, protection, and sacrificial love. So, let Christ's loyal love for you set the standard for how you love yourself and others.

Greater love hath no man than this, that a man lay down his life for his friends. Ye are my friends, if ye do whatsoever I command you. Henceforth I call you not servants; for the servant knoweth not what his lord doeth: but I have called you friends; for all things that I have heard of my Father I have made known unto you.
John 15:13-15

CHAPTER 2

7 Reasons Men Must Say "YES" to a Relationship with God

Everyone in life has a purpose. When God calls you, He calls you out of something into something even greater. If you look around you, you will see everything that God is calling you from. When God called Moses, He came to him in the form of a burning bush. When God called Apostle Paul, He knocked him off his high horse—literally. How about you? How do you want God to call you? One thing for sure, He may not show you a burning bush or knock you off a horse, but God will send you a preacher. From the time of John the Baptist to present, God used man to reach one other. Oh yes, His signs and wonders are even greater in the church now through His servants. The way the gospel of Jesus Christ has reached you is through teaching and discipleship, and even through this book. Jesus taught us how to do discipleship well. He called the 12, taught them, and then,sent them to reach others.

Go ye therefore, and teach all nations, baptizing them in the name of the Father, and of the Son, and of the Holy Ghost: Teaching them to observe all things whatsoever I have commanded you: and, lo, I am with you always, even unto the end of the world. Amen. Matthew 28:19-20

When you answer the call of God on your life, it will be the most important decision you will ever make, with everything to win and nothing to lose. When you walk away from sin and surrender your life to Jesus, the peace and the love of God will overtake you. This is the most beautiful feeling; nothing on this earth can ever come close to this feeling that we receive when we embrace our salvation in Jesus Christ. Here are seven reasons that should help you make this decision today:

1. Saying yes to God will ensure your name is written in the Book of Life and

receive salvation. Be baptized of water
and of the Holy Spirit.

2. Giving your life to Christ will not remove
   all the troubles in your life, but He will
   teach you how to confront and demolish
   them. No matter how bad your life has
   been, the blood of Jesus has the power
   to reset your life and give you a new
   start.

3. When you build a relationship with God,
   your relationship is not just for you, but
   also for your family. The power of God
   moves through your family to those who
   are sick and delivers those who need
   deliverance.

4. Until you answer the call of God on your
   life, you will continue to live like a roller
   coaster. The fight is not a fight you can
   fight in the physical. You need Jesus to
   fight the spiritual battles for you.

5. When Jesus enters your life, you
   become a new being. The old things are
   gone. Sickness is gone, addictions are
   gone, even sin no longer has power
   over you.

6. When you make Jesus the God of your
    life, you receive the power to become a
    son of God. The Spirit of God will enter
    you and empower you to cast out devils
    and heal the sick.
7. Saying yes to the call of God on your life
    will break every generational curse in
    your life and your children's lives. For
    example, breast cancer is a
    generational curse, but when God
    anoints you, nothing can touch you or
    your children.

*And it shall come to pass in that day, that his
burden shall be taken away from off thy
shoulder, and his yoke from off thy neck, and
the yoke shall be destroyed because of the
anointing.*
Isaiah 10:27

*Therefore if any man be in Christ, he is a new
creature: old things are passed away; behold,
all things are become new.*
2 Corinthians 5:17

Four Ways to Break Every Curse

Every man will always find himself in one season or another. Fruit comes in specific seasons. If you plant, you must plant in the right seasons in order for your seeds to grow. Harvest comes in specific seasons. Where you are in your season is dictated by four things:

1. Your words: When you speak, you prophesy. Through your words, you declare peace or chaos, healing or sickness, bondage or freedom, poverty or riches. So, when I hear someone who is sick and they say "my" migraine, "my" fever, "my" prostate cancer, my, my, my…. I hear a level of ignorance. When you take such a high level of possession over any sickness, it has no reason to leave you. Sickness is a spirit. You need to speak to it by its name and command it to go. It is not your migraine, but it is "a" headache that must go out of your body. The reason they call it a migraine is because it's a chronic pain that keeps returning. You can use your words and the authority given to you by God to rebuke it. When you know the power of your words, God

will dictate your season, health or sickness.
The same is true for every other area of your
life. When you empower yourself through the
studying of the Word, prayer and worship, your
words can and will become a weapon against
the enemy.

*Death and life are in the power of the tongue:
and they that love it shall eat the fruit thereof.*
Proverbs 18:21

*For as he thinketh in his heart, so is he: Eat
and drink, saith he to thee; but his heart is not
with thee.*
Proverbs 23:7

2. Your Position: Where are you now? As a
man, you don't belong everywhere. Be careful
with your involvement. Many men missed their
appointed times and places with God because
of their association. The breaking of
generational curses may even require you to
move geographically because a man doesn't
thrive everywhere.
Adam missed his appointment with God.

And they heard the voice of the Lord God
walking in the garden in the cool of the day:
and Adam and his wife hid themselves from
the presence of the Lord God amongst the
trees of the garden.
Genesis 3:8-11

The cool of the day was Adam's appointed time
with God, and the Garden was the appointed
place.

And the Lord God called unto Adam, and said
unto him, Where art thou?
Genesis 3:9

Bishop L. Style III helped clarified that God was
more disappointed with Adam's missing his
appointment with Him than He was about his
sin.

And he said, I heard thy voice in the garden,
and I was afraid, because I was naked; and I
hid myself.
Genesis 3:10

Sometimes, shame from sinning will cause you
to hide from the presence of God.
*And he said, Who told thee that thou wast
naked? Hast thou eaten of the tree, whereof I
commanded thee that thou shouldest not eat?
Genesis 3:11*

God asked Adam a question. This key question
is still relevant today. "Who told you…?" Who
told you that you could no longer be a valuable
member of God's kingdom because of your
shortcomings? You need to know that God is
so interested in your future that He is not
looking at your past. Forgive yourself, repent
and be baptized for the remission of your sins.
Today can be your day of repositioning.
Regardless of your situation, the devil has no
power over your life. You are not your
mistakes. Thank God you went through some
of the things you went through. They were all
lessons. Now, go and enter a discipleship
training program in your church to be
equipped, because there are millions who are
about to go through what you have gone
through. God has prepared you to teach them

and share your testimony.

Positioning, in this context, is not a hypothetical place. It is a literal place of rendezvous with God. While this may be different in some situations, for many, your positioning is in your church and during your service times. It is literally the place where God has placed you to be developed, pruned and matured. There, He will send people who have gone through the hardships of life just to rescue you, teach you and prepare you for ministry; this is similar to how He used Moses for the children of Israel. Your service times are extremely important at your church. These are set times in place for you and God. It doesn't matter what happens during the week, we know that we will be at church for Tuesday night bible study and for worship on Sunday morning. God will use your pastor to invite a guest speaker who is anointed in the area of healing, and because you honored your appointed place and time, He will pray for your wife today and she will be healed.

Every powerful man in the Bible had an

encounter with someone God sent to take him into his next season. God will not appear before you like He did with Adam, but He will always send you someone to teach, pray and counsel you.

As a bird that wandereth from her nest, so is a man that wandereth from his place.
Proverbs 27:8

3. Relationship: Your friendships and marriage will cancel one other out if you don't select carefully. Many marriages have failed because of ungodly friendships, and many men have walked away from their relationship with God because of ungodly marriages. Though many have tried to apply faith when dealing with people, the correct method is to use wisdom when dealing with people and use faith for God. A toxic relationship will destroy you and your marriage if you don't come out of it. However, a great friend will help you to restore and strengthen your marriage.
A man must be selective when choosing relationships. The word "no" is an acceptable

answer to more than half of what you will be asked to do during the course of your day. A man's words should be few. Again, use wisdom for people and faith for God. It is wise to wait three seconds (count to three) to gather your thoughts before you respond in a conversation.

Whoso is partner with a thief hateth his own soul: he heareth cursing, and bewrayeth it not. Proverbs 29:24

Your marriage is the only earthly relationship that God created for you (the man), and He let the man (no one else) be in charge of it, even today. While your pastor may counsel you, the man is ultimately responsible for making sure that his marriage is well, even to the point of giving himself for his wife. You are a flesh and spiritual shield protecting your wife at all times. **Never leave your wife and children behind for the purpose of ministry because your first ministry is at home. Anything else is in error.**

*Husbands, love your wives, even as Christ also
loved the church, and gave himself for it.
Ephesians 5:25*

Divorce, in the church, is an abomination. If the
sons, fathers, and grandfathers in a family tree
are having trouble staying married, that is a
generational curse that must be addressed and
broken. Marriage is an institution created by
God. Therefore, the enemy is relentless in his
fight to destroy it. You must guard your
marriage against any ambush. All strikes
against your marriage are temporary. **Never
make a permanent decision for a temporary
situation.**

The very nature of a man of God is that he is
wise. He is mature in the things of man and a
faithful student in the things of God. A faithful
man with no wisdom will be well on his way to
heaven, but he will die poor, miserable, lonely
and hungry on this earth. This shall not be your
portion, in Jesus' Name.

Wisdom is the principal thing; therefore get

*wisdom: and with all thy getting get
understanding.*
Proverbs 4:7

*Whoso loveth wisdom rejoiceth his father: but
he that keepeth company with harlots spendeth
his substance.*
Proverbs 29:3

4. Your Seeds: Your words are seeds planted;
they will eventually become substance. Every
seed that is planted will have a harvest, and
everyone will reap the harvest of their seeds.
Your seeds are a part of you. It's the legacy
you built. It is the brand you created.

Eleven Facts about Seeds

1. Seeds are purposely set aside.
2. Only the best products can be seeds.
3. The seeds you planted indicate the
   harvest you will reap.
4. In order to reap a harvest, you must
   plant a seed.
5. No seed is the same.

6. Everyone has one or more seeds.
7. Only expectations make seeds grow.
8. Only two things happen to seeds: you either plant or you eat them.
9. The quality of your seed is in your expectations.
10. Every seed has a seed within it.
11. Seeds need fertile ground to grow.

Generational curses come from four places

Self-Curse

A man who is lacking wisdom speaks in and out of season with no fear of consequences, but a man full of wisdom makes his words few. When he speaks, he releases blessings. His words bring pleasure to those who listen to his voice. His life is full of grace and longevity. He speaks life and nations listen when his mouth is open. His words bring prosperity to him, and his children find favor at the gates of the city for every word he ever speaks returns life to his bosom. He understands and applies the discipline of silence, for they are of utmost

importance to him. He masters discipline and
prefers it over anger.

Death and life are in the power of the tongue:
and they that love it shall eat the fruit thereof.
Proverbs 18:21

But the tongue can no man tame; it is an unruly
evil, full of deadly poison.
James 3:8

He that keepeth his mouth keepeth his life: but
he that openeth wide his lips shall have
destruction.
Proverbs 13:3

Cursed by Parents

The curse of dishonor is the only chastisement
that your parents have no control over. If you
have not honored your parents in obedience,
you have called judgment to your life. The
Bible tells us to honor our parents. This is the
only one of the Ten Commandments that
comes with a built-in promise; this is because

the curse is already in those who dishonor their parents.

Honor thy father and mother; (which is the first commandment with promise;) That it may be well with thee, and thou mayest live long on the earth.
Ephesians 6:2-3

The eye that mocketh at his father, and despiseth to obey his mother, the ravens of the valley shall pick it out, and the young eagles shall eat it.
Proverbs 30:17

Curse Put on You by Someone Else

Words carry spirits. When someone speaks against you, that person practically predicts the future for you and releases a demon that you now have to fight. You should be familiar with the words **receive** and **rebuke**. When someone blesses you, you receive it by saying thank you or amen. Likewise, when someone curses you, if you don't agree, you need to disagree by rebuking the said declaration. These are what we call "social norms." When someone says "good morning" or "have a blessed day," it is socially expected for you to receive and give back a "good morning" or a "thank you! You too." This is what we call good manners. Society loves those with good manners and rebukes those with bad manners. When looking at it in the spiritual realm, you need to "rebuke" people who have bad manners or people who are ignorant. **Example (Curse)**: Don't let your son go to Harvard University; he wouldn't make it. I heard only fifty percent of Black students graduate. **Your (Rebuke):** I rebuke you with this statement. My son will be one of the fifty percent who graduated from Harvard with a 4.0 GPA.

Answer a fool according to his folly, lest he be wise in his own conceit.
Proverbs 26:5

Note: It is not bad manners to rebuke a person. What you receive or rebuke will dictate the future battles you will face. Open rebuke is

better than secret love (Proverbs 27:5).
My prayer is that you have surrounded yourself
with wisdom and counsel. You shall separate
yourself from the unwise, the unlearned and
the ungodly so that the words spoken over you
and your family are words of blessing, in Jesus'
name. Amen.

Generational Curses and Reversal

In many cases, generational curses are a
contract entered into knowingly or unknowingly
by someone in your family's bloodline
hundreds of years ago. A curse can also come
from rebelling against God.

*Therefore thus saith the Lord; Behold, I will
punish Shemaiah the Nehelamite, and his
seed: he shall not have a man to dwell among
this people; neither shall he behold the good
that I will do for my people, saith the Lord;
because he hath taught rebellion against the
Lord.*
Jeremiah 29.32

**Every generational curse is reversible. The
blood of Jesus is able to wash away all sins
and purify all things.**

*Therefore if any man be in Christ, he is a new
creature: old things are passed away; behold,
all things are become new.*
II Corinthians 5:17

I urge you, do not stay in the same position.
You can change your trajectory by making
Jesus Christ your God and Savior. Up till now,
you're probably asking, "How will I know if my
family is operating under a curse?" Well, it's all
around you. Diabetes is a curse that can affect
an entire generation. Your mother,
grandmother, and great-grandmother have all
died from it, and now you have started
worrying about dying from the disease. Your
doctor called it genetic because it is sickness
that affected the women on your family tree.
Your doctor asked you a few questions about
your family, and from there, he concluded that
you will suffer that same sickness by the time
you are thirty years of age.

39

Your answer: In your softest, most humble voice say, "Doctor, I rebuke you and that sickness in the name of Jesus. I am a new creature washed by the blood of Jesus. What followed my family will not follow me. The old things have gone away. I have been made new. I will not have diabetes."

I have seen some families where every woman in the family has suffered from breast cancer, and they were all dead by the time they were forty-years old. I have seen some other families where every man has died of a heart attack by the time they were fifty-years old. There are some families where every one of their firstborn children have died at birth. I have seen so many families where all the men have gone to jail. In certain families, all the women were divorced by the age forty. These things have become the new social norm, but I am here to tell you that they are not normal. Jesus can change your story today.

CHAPTER 3

Understanding Legacy

Every man is his own brand. If you were to die today, what will you be best known for? Anything that will disappear after your death is not a legacy. Legacy lives after you have stopped living. Your ministry, your friends, your children are all part of your legacy. Your legacy is tied to your destiny. A man who is operating in his destiny has a place and time of fellowship with God; this is where godly legacies are built, both with family and community.

Ten Keys to Help Restore Spiritual Legacy

1. Never worship without your spouse.
2. Be sensitive to the voice of God and discern the voice of people.

3. Nourish your spouse with the Word of God.
4. Be the priest of your house.
5. Obey the instructions that God has given you.
6. Have the willingness to be counseled and pastored.
7. Tithe in everything, including your time.
8. Attend services at your church.
9. Pray for your pastor(s).
10. Protect your place of fellowship.

Seven Ways to Build Legacy Through Relationship

Relationships with your wife, husband, father, mother, children and friends are necessary to building a legacy.

Below, you'll find the recipe that will bring you the results you've desired through these relationships.

1. Take good care of yourself.
2. Love on your family.
3. Raise your children in the things of God.

4. Cultivate your seeds.
5. Forgive without retaliation.
6. Know when to let go.
7. Be constant in seeking Godly counsel.

Twelve Ways to Guard Your Legacy

1. Guard your children.
2. Guard your ministry.
3. Guard your relationships.
4. Guard your wisdom.
5. Guard your counsel.
6. Guard your followership.
7. Guard your love.
8. Guard your stewardship.
9. Guard your discipleship.
10. Guard your words.

Let your speech be alway with grace, seasoned with salt, that ye may know how ye ought to answer every man. Colossians 4:6

11. Guard your soul winning.
12. Guard your faith.

All of these keys to your legacy need to be guarded because the enemy is constantly working to destroy them. No man can have a legacy on earth unless these twelve keys are in order. How do you identify toxic relationships? Certain people display the characteristics of a friend, but they are agents of the devil. They willingly turned their backs on God and embraced the work of Satan, thus allowing themselves to become agents of Satan. While you are praying for someone to change, you have to understand that if they are not in a relationship with Christ, they are in a relationship with Satan. When it comes to spiritual things, there is no such thing as being neutral. If you are not guided by the Spirit of God, you are then an empty vessel for the devil to occupy. Every man has some toxic relationships that he must let go of.

In order to identify a toxic relationship you have to:

1. Identify the kind of person you are dealing with. Look at their behavior to see what occupies their time. Listen to the words they speak. Remember, the word of the man will identify the man.

2. Get to know the person's motives. Look for reciprocity in the relationship.
3. Take the time to get to know yourself. It is possible that you are the toxic one in the relationship. Take action and seek counsel immediately.

The Two Types of People in This World

1. **A giver -** A giver is one who is operating in the assignment of giving. God has blessed them and gave them the heart of the giver. Every man has had an encounter with a giver. You will have some givers for an assignment. They come in a season of your life to give and to assist you through a specific situation in your life. When you meet a giver, be humble, thank God, and thank them. Show gratitude and celebrate the giver in your life because they are often not around forever. Whatever you honor/praise will multiply in your life. Take good notes so that you too will become a giver. The more you give, the

more you multiply; this is what I call "overflow".

2. **A taker** – A taker is the opposite of a giver. They only come to suck you dry—period. They are parasites looking for a weak person to prey on. You will not know this at first because they start with "having a need", but that "need" will never go away. You have to pray for wisdom to discern the spirit of the person. A taker will always seem to have a particular need every time they meet you. When in doubt, wait seven days, the need will somehow solve itself, expire or 'magically' disappear.

Four Ways to Get to Know Someone

1. **Hire them** – When you hire someone who is in need, that person will display gratitude through his or her performance. They will display urgency with a purpose. Either way, the reverse of these things will display their character.

2. **Marry them** – "Only those who sleep with Joe really knows Joe." You can never fully know someone, because everyone you see is wearing a mask— not in the literal sense, but someone's life experiences, rejection and disappointments will cause them to display their character. This is why I encourage everyone who is getting married or planning to get married to sit down with a Certified SCLU Counselor and undergo a temperament profile review. This would allow them to get to know each other.

3. **Tell them a secret** – The United States federal government has classes of clearance level for individuals based on how much they believe they can be trusted. Sharing a secret with someone is the best way to get to know that person. What people do after you have told them that they are the only ones with the information you have just shared with them will amaze you.

4. **Say "NO" to them** – One of the true

ways to test someone's character is to tell them "no." One of the most chaotic conflicts you may have with a spouse, child, or a friend is when you tell them no. Their selfishness will be on display when you sit back and observe their behavior.

Who are You?

When you get to know yourself, you open the door for better intimate relationships, both with God and with people. Knowing who you are gives authority to your identity and helps you to better understand your limitations. Reconcile yourself under sonship with God.

But as many as received him, to them gave he power to become the sons of God, even to them that believe on his name: Which were born, not of blood, nor of the will of the flesh, nor of the will of man, but of God.
John 1:12-13

The Giraffe and the Turtle

A turtle doesn't have the same perspective as a giraffe. A turtle sees things from a very low perspective. A giraffe sees things from a very high perspective. They are both very honest within their perspective.

A chicken cannot be intimate with an eagle because chickens are domesticated and eat from the ground. The eagle carries its food into the air to enjoy the meal, regardless of where it got the food from. God created you to live like an eagle. Isaiah 40:31 says, *But they that wait upon the Lord shall renew their strength; they shall mount up with wings as eagles; they shall run, and not be weary; and they shall walk, and not faint.* When you surround yourself with the people of yesterday, they keep pulling you back to what you used to be. But, when you have met with your destiny helpers, they are interested in your dreams. A giraffe has a 25-pound heart that pumps blood to and through its long neck, allowing it to stand tall. If it lowers its head to the level of the turtle, it will die. God has created you to stand tall. You will endanger your position if you lower your perspective.

Three Things That Will Lower Your Perspective

1. **Having the wrong friends** – Friendship is necessary for a man. However, the kind of friend you choose will determine the future you create.

Ointment and perfume rejoice the heart: so doth the sweetness of a man's friend by hearty counsel.
Proverbs 27:9

Walk with the wise and become wise, for companion of fools suffers harm.
Proverbs 13:20

2. **Listening to the wrong teaching or counseling** – Your hearing is the number one defense for your faith. Your faith is strengthened or weakened by what you hear. Listening to the wrong

teaching will destroy your faith.

So then faith cometh by hearing, and hearing
by the word of God.
Romans 10:17

3. **Entering into a wrong relationship –**
   Every man's destiny is tied to the wife
   he chooses. God has delivered divine
   powers to marriage. Your authority rests
   in the power of unity.

Again I say unto you, That if two of you shall
agree on earth as touching anything that they
shall ask, it shall be done for them of my
Father which is in heaven.
Matthew 18:19

Who can find a virtuous woman? For her price
is far above rubies. The heart of her husband
doth safely trust in her, so that he shall have no
need of spoil.
Proverbs 31:10-11

The Three Types of People You Will Meet in

Life

A man should always have friends. It is part of a having fellowship. Relationships are vital to everything, both in ministry and in the secular world. Having the right relationships, however, is totally dependent on your ability to identify character. Every friendship is not the same. Motive will help to identify someone's personality. A person's life experiences will draw them to you because you have been positioned to take them to where they want to go or what they will become. These people are in your circle right now. Here are three types of friends a man has.

1. A Constituent is someone who is trustworthy and faithful to you. They have the characteristics of a perfect friend. They are loyal, but their friendship with you is conditional upon you maintaining your status, both socially and economically. They are with you because of what you stand for and your position. A Constituent will leave you if you lose your job or change your position.

2. A Comrade is someone who will take a

bullet for you. Your existence is extremely important to them. They will feed you and babysit your children. They will be there for you until the end of the fight. They will hunt down anyone or anything that threatens you. But they are only with you because you both have a common enemy. Do not mistake this type of relationship for a friendship. A comrade has no problem turning on you after you both have destroyed the common enemy. The sad truth is, some men have even married their comrades.

3. A Confidant is a true friend. They don't count what you do or don't have. A Confidant is someone whose friendship you can count on. The people you have allowed in your life will dictate the future you create for yourself. Some people may come and take away, others may serve as givers to your life, and some people may not be takers, they simply may not have anything to give. Nevertheless, they come into your life to help you build a better you. A Confidant is a covenant partner for life.

CHAPTER 4

The Love, Marriage & Sex Ministry

The Love Test

Everyone will undergo the love test. If you haven't gone through it, you are going through it right now. If not, you will soon. The loophole of love doesn't exist. There is no way to love without being selfless.

For this cause I bow my knees unto the Father of our Lord Jesus Christ, Of whom the whole family in heaven and earth is named, That he would grant you, according to the riches of his glory, to be strengthened with might by his Spirit in the inner man; That Christ may dwell in your hearts by faith; that ye, being rooted and grounded in love, May be able to comprehend with all saints what is the breadth,

and length, and depth, and height; And to know the love of Christ, which passeth knowledge, that ye might be filled with all the fullness of God. Now unto him that is able to do exceeding abundantly above all that we ask or think, according to the power that worketh in us.
Ephesians 3:14-20

Everyone's love will be tested. You don't have to pass it, but you will take the test. God has favored you. He will take you through life and expose you to teachings every step of the way. Though you may not understand it now, everything you have been through has been a test for greatness. You are still here. It did not kill you because these assessments are tests of knowledge.

For our light affliction, which is but for a moment, worketh for us a far more exceeding and eternal weight of glory.
2 Corinthians 4:17

Teaching

The love test is for those who have been taught for the purpose of strengthening the inner man. It doesn't matter how strong and beautiful you are on the outside, there are somethings in life that will tickle your weakness. Our Lord, Jesus wants to transform your weaknesses into strengths, exposing your hands to combat and building your calluses for the work ahead.

Therefore I take pleasure in infirmities, in reproaches, in necessities, in persecutions, in distresses for Christ's sake: for when I am weak, then am I strong.
2 Corinthians 12:10

The Test
With a test comes the potential to have the wrong answer. It is not a test if it doesn't give you choices. What choices are you facing today? How you respond to the choices in life determines your readiness for promotion. You are being tested because you are real. Jesus was tested in three different areas:

1. **The test of provision** – Man of God, be

aware of the test of provision. The devil will come to you at your moment of apparent need. I use 'apparent' because it only appears to be a need. You need to understand that God has already brought you through the hard times, and He will never forsake you—NOT EVER.

And when the tempter came to him, he said, If thou be the Son of God, command that these stones be made bread.
But he answered and said, It is written, Man shall not live by bread alone, but by every word that proceedeth out of the mouth of God.
Matthew 4:3-4

2. **The test of protection** – One of the greatest challenges for a man is to know when to take his hands off a situation and just let Jesus take care of him. It is in a man's nature to muscle himself through his own security. The devil will try to use the power God gives you to test you. It is better to use the scriptures to rebuke Satan. It is better to

understand this; just because you can do something doesn't mean you should do it. At who's command anyway? The devil doesn't have any authority to command your actions. Train your ears to be sensitive to the voice of God and God alone.

Then the devil taketh him up into the holy city, and setteth him on a pinnacle of the temple, and saith unto him, If thou be the Son of God, cast thyself down: for it is written, He shall give his angels charge concerning thee: and in their hands they shall bear thee up, lest at any time thou dash thy foot against a stone. Jesus said unto him, It is written again, Thou shalt not tempt the Lord thy God.
Matthew 4:5-7

My sheep hear my voice, and I know them, and they follow me:
John 10:27

And a stranger will they not follow, but will flee from him: for they know not the voice of

strangers.
John 10:5

3. **The Test of Power** – Self-restraint is another powerful discipline that's necessary for a man to have. The love for fame and power has destroyed families and rendered many men powerless. The devil doesn't give anything that doesn't come with negative consequences. Everything the devil has ever offered you was something that God has already given you or something He was preparing you for a set time. Whatever the devil offers you is a cheap trade-off for something greater. He sees your destiny. True fame and power can come only from God and it will give glory back to Him. God's gift is eternal. His gifts come in specific seasons. He has been preparing you your entire life to receive and exercise the authority and dominion He has given you through Christ.

Again, the devil taketh him up into an exceeding high mountain, and sheweth him all the kingdoms of the world, and the glory of them, And saith unto him, All these things will I give thee, if thou wilt fall down and worship me. Then saith Jesus unto him, Get thee hence, Satan: for it is written, Thou shalt worship the Lord thy God, and him only shalt thou serve.
Matthew 4:8-10

The best part about this scripture is what happened after Jesus rebuked the devil. When Satan tried tempting Jesus and failed, the scripture says he departed from Jesus and God's angels came and ministered unto Him. I pray for you even now—As you have survived every temptation of the devil, he shall depart from you, your wife, your children and your ministry. And the angels of God shall come and minister to your family, in the name of Jesus. Amen!

Then the devil leaveth him, and, behold, angels came and ministered unto him.
Matthew 4:11

The "Fish Love"

It was a calm Friday evening. I sat inside a small restaurant while I was on vacation at Mole, St. Nicolas, Haiti. The waitress came to our table and asked what I wanted for dinner. "Fried fish, please," I replied. About twelve minutes later, out came a big white oval platter with a whole fish, fried with a lime wedge in the center of the plate. I picked the fish up with my two thumbs and index fingers and started to bite away. My brother-in law gave me "that look" from across the table. He clearly wanted to say something, but he was too busy chewing on fried plantains and pikliz to say anything. "**I love fish**," I passively stated while I continued to eat away at the fish.

The next day, as we drove past the little restaurant on our way to the airport, I was still reminiscing about the "I love fish" statement. Gosh…I prayed that my love for my God and my neighbor would be better than my "fish love." It would be ungodly of me to not be consciously aware of how I love my neighbor. I can't do anything to God because He is God, but I saw what I could do to the fish I claimed to love. It was then official. I need to revisit my heart concerning how I love.

Jesus is a man's role model for love. He literally gave His life so that I can live. How can I love like Jesus? I know how we love the fish; we took a live fish from its habitat and lured it onto a hook. We pulled it outside of its natural habitat, allowing it to suffocate to death. We put spices on it that make it smell, look, and taste good. We heat up oil to 350 degrees and fry it for 7-10 minutes. We do all of these things because we "love fish." It's crazy, right? Are you saying it is not the same kind of love? Did you know that people are getting married with this kind of love today? If you look at television and the news reports in 2018 alone, you'll find that "selfish love" has driven husbands to murder their wives and children. Mothers have even murdered their children and husbands, all in the name of love. Jesus said:

Thou shalt love the Lord thy God with all thy heart, and with all thy soul, and with all thy mind. This is the first and great commandment. And the second is like unto it, Thou shalt love thy neighbour as thyself. Matthew 22:37-39

Giving is a commitment to love, and love is a commitment to investment. If you are confused by this statement, it's because just "love" wasn't meant to finish a statement all on its own. You can begin with giving, but you will finish with investment. The only thing you get in return is love. Man struggled with love because he has a problem with giving. Love gives, and if it's not unconditional, it is not all love. Giving has always been a heart issue because when a man refuses to give, he refuses to commit to love. Jesus committed all the way to the cross to pay for our sins. Love is a selfless heart engagement.

For as the Father hath life in himself; so hath he given to the Son to have life in himself. John 5:26.

I am the living bread which came down from

heaven: if any man eat of this bread, he shall live forever: and the bread that I will give is my flesh, which I will give for the life of the world. John 6:51

Giving to Your Neighbor

Anyone who is a giver is also a seed bearer. If God has burdened you with a desire to give, He is calling you to advance His Kingdom on this earth. When you give to the least among us, Jesus says you give to Him. Remember, a giver's hands are blessed and lacking nothing.

For I was an hungred, and ye gave me meat: I was thirsty, and ye gave me drink: I was a stranger, and ye took me in:Naked, and ye clothed me: I was sick, and ye visited me: I was in prison, and ye came unto me.
Then shall the righteous answer him, saying, Lord, when saw we thee an hungred, and fed thee? or thirsty, and gave thee drink?
When saw we thee a stranger, and took thee in? or naked, and clothed thee?
Or when saw we thee sick, or in prison, and

came unto thee?
And the King shall answer and say unto them,
Verily I say unto you, Inasmuch as ye have
done it unto one of the least of these my
brethren, ye have done it unto me.
Matthew 25:35-40

It is all fine that you were given an envelope and asked to give cheerfully. So, do you tithe under the system where the greater the music, the better you dance and the more your tithes increase? NO. As a minister of the gospel, what I pray for and hope to see is that these things are coming from the heart.

Every man according as he purposeth in his
heart, so let him give; not grudgingly, or of
necessity: for God loveth a cheerful giver.
2 Corinthians 9:7

Giving is a Heart Issue

The problem is the heart is attached to a head and the head is not thinking the way the Bible teaches it to think. So, we have a heart that is not connected to the head. When the tithe envelope is given, the music is great, the choir is singing and dancing, it is all done so that you are provoked to give cheerfully. You don't want to find yourself tipping God. Whatsoever you have in your heart to contribute to God's Kingdom, put it aside in advance. Let it not be the first thing you see when you open your wallets.

You may say, I don't know if I understand the "GIVING THING"! Well, as a Teacher of the Word, I have got to help the heart by ministering to the head. Imagine the world's population was a minuscule one hundred people. Seventy of them don't know Christ, thirty of them do know Christ, thirty are whites, and seventy are from other ethnicities. Fifty-one of them are women and 49 of them are men. Eighty of the one hundred live in substandard housing with no running water. Fifty of them are malnourished with only one meal, maybe daily. Seventy of them can't read. One child under ten years of age is dying right now from malnutrition. Six of them have over half of the world population's income and the six percent represent America.

If you are the dad of the child who is dying, what is the possibility of the dad saying to one the six percent, "Please help! My child is dying"? Now, imagine what the rest of the six percent are doing with the abundance of income. Some are preoccupied with their positions of wealth. They don't have time to listen to the cries for help. Let's use the dollar for example. Twenty-four cents is set aside for the cost of housing, 19 cents for the cost of healthcare, 22 cents for the cost of recreational needs and pleasure, 15 cents for the cost of food, 17 cents for an automobile. So, do we have anything left at all to give to the dad whose son is dying? If you do the math, the rich dad only has two cents left. He might have to tell the poor dad, "Your son is going to have to die." Shocking? Yes! I have just described to you our world, the way it is right now.

This is what our missionaries face in the field every day. Once they have been exposed to this overwhelming fact, they have dedicated their lives to changing it. Your head may be

saying something else to you at this moment, but I want you to connect this with your heart. If you have preoccupied your dollar and there is not enough to help others, it is a problem for the church (you) because that dollar looks like the dollar in your pocket right now.
No one wants to FIX this problem, because IT IS THE AMERICAN WAY. Yet, somehow, you are right now in financial trouble. Not only do you have enough, you are praying to God, "Please give me more; I am in need." GOD DOES NOT REWARD BAD BEHAVIOR. A man who is a good steward at managing God's blessing is never lacking.

*Give, and it shall be given unto you; good measure, pressed down, and shaken together, and **running over**, shall men give into your bosom. For with the same measure that ye mete withal it shall be measured to you again. Luke 6:38*

Bring ye all the tithes into the storehouse, that there may be meat in mine house, and prove me now herewith, saith the LORD of hosts, if I

will not open you the windows of heaven, and pour you out a blessing, that there shall not be room enough to receive it.
Malachi 3:10

CHAPTER 5

Marriage

God created the heavens, the earth, and everything in it. He saw that it was very good. Out of everything God created, the only imperfection He saw was that it was not good for man to be alone, so He created the woman for him. Loneliness is a curse that has to be broken. The order of creation was so that every man has for himself a wife. Marriage is a divine union created by God for a man and his whomman.

And the Lord God said, It is not good that the man should be alone; I will make him a help meet for him.
Genesis 2:18

1. Man's loneliness is a danger to himself. When a wife and husband are praying

together, their prayers in unity gives
them power and their labor will not be in vain.
No matter where you are in the world, a man
and his wife can become an economic
powerhouse when they work together.

*Two are better than one; because they have a
good reward for their labor. For if they fall, the
one will lift up his fellow: but woe to him that is
alone when he falleth; for he hath not another
to help him up.*
Ecclesiastes 4:9-10

2. **God gives deliverance to the power
   of two -** Brother, I encourage you to
   stay in the unity of agreement with your
   wife, spiritually, physically, and
   emotionally. Pray for your wife because
   your spouse is the first person the devil
   will attack; this is because your union is
   a threat to his kingdom. Your marriage
   comes with power and authority.

*Verily I say unto you, Whatsoever ye shall bind
on earth shall be bound in heaven: and*

*whatsoever ye shall loose on earth shall be
loosed in heaven. Again I say unto you, That if
two of you shall agree on earth as touching
anything that they shall ask, it shall be done.
Matthew 18:18-19*

*For where two or three are gathered together
in my name, there am I in the midst of them. for
them of my Father which is in heaven.
Matthew 18:20*

3. **Jesus promoted a 2x2 corporation.**
   As we see in scripture, God always
   released His disciples into the field in
   pairs; never alone. We are relational
   beings. We need social interactions.
   Working in the field of ministry for years
   and never marrying was never the plan
   of God for us.

*And he called unto him the twelve, and began
to send them forth by two and two; and gave
them power over unclean spirits.
Mark 6:7*

And when they came nigh to Jerusalem, unto Bethphage and Bethany, at the mount of Olives, he sendeth forth two of his disciples, And saith unto them, Go your way into the village over against you: and as soon as ye be entered into it, ye shall find a colt tied, whereon never man sat; loose him, and bring him . And if any man say unto you, Why do ye this? say ye that the Lord hath need of him; and straightway he will send him hither.
Mark 11:1-3

And he sendeth forth two of his disciples, and saith unto them, Go ye into the city, and there shall meet you a man bearing a pitcher of water: follow him. And wheresoever he shall go in, say ye to the goodman of the house, The Master saith, Where is the guestchamber, where I shall eat the Passover with my disciples? And he will shew you a large upper room furnished and prepared: there make ready for us.
Mark 14:13-15

This is the third time I am coming to you. In the

mouth of two or three witnesses shall every word be established.
2 Corinthians 13:1

4. **Togetherness** - the combined effect is greater than the sum of their separate effects.

And when the day of Pentecost was fully come, they were all with one accord in one place. And suddenly there came a sound from heaven as of a rushing mighty wind, and it filled all the house where they were sitting. And there appeared unto them cloven tongues like as of fire, and it sat upon each of them. And they were all filled with the Holy Ghost, and began to speak with other tongues, as the Spirit gave them utterance.
Acts 2:1-4

Behold, how good and how pleasant it is for brethren to dwell together in unity!
Psalm 133:1

With all lowliness and meekness, with

*longsuffering, forbearing one another in love;
Endeavouring to keep the unity of the Spirit in
the bond of peace.There is one body, and one
Spirit, even as ye are called in one hope of
your calling;
Ephesians 4:2-4*

*And he gave some, apostles; and some,
prophets; and some, evangelists; and some,
pastors and teachers; For the perfecting of the
saints, for the work of the ministry, for the
edifying of the body of Christ: Till we all come
in the unity of the faith, and of the knowledge of
the Son of God, unto a perfect man, unto the
measure of the stature of the fulness of Christ.
Ephesians 4:11-13*

CHAPTER 6

The Burden Of Relationships

Ending Proverbs 31 Ministries in the Church

The burden of a relationship has been and will always be conferred to the woman. Even when man was separated from God, he found a way to blame it on the woman.

And he said, Who told thee that thou wast naked? Hast thou eaten of the tree, whereof I commanded thee that thou shouldest not eat? And the man said, The woman whom thou gavest to be with me, she gave me of the tree, and I did eat.
Genesis 3:11-12

In reality, every power was given unto man from God; even the power to protect his wife.

Adam sinned; sin brought shame to him, and his shame caused him to hide from the presence of God.

Now the serpent was more subtil than any beast of the field which the Lord God had made. And he said unto the woman, Yea, hath God said, Ye shall not eat of every tree of the garden? And the woman said unto the serpent, We may eat of the fruit of the trees of the garden: But of the fruit of the tree which is in the midst of the garden, God hath said, Ye shall not eat of it, neither shall ye touch it, lest ye die. And the serpent said unto the woman, Ye shall not surely die: For God doth know that in the day ye eat thereof, then your eyes shall be opened, and ye shall be as gods, knowing good and evil.
Genesis 3:1-5

Adam's first failure was his absence in his marriage. The serpent led his wife in a long conversation in his absence. One can argue that God hadn't spoken to Eve and had given no instructions directly to her, nevertheless, He spoke to her husband. Adam's responsibility was to teach her the laws of God.

God's order needs to be restored in our families today, even though man hasn't regained full control and authority. God is looking to restore the same level of intimacy with men that He had with Adam, but women everywhere have been chasing God, while men have served as deadweights on their backs. The women have been plagued by the burden of relationship that is placed on them by their men. You can almost see divorce settlements everywhere; the man blames the woman, even in cases where he was engaged in extramarital affairs. No matter what the man does, the woman must remain pure. Even though man has attempted to fix his heart with women, it has been ineffective because he must fix his heart to God first.

Blessed are they that keep his testimonies, and that seek him with the whole heart.
Psalm 119:2

You cannot seek God with half of your heart. A

man without his woman is a halfhearted man,
and he who is without God is no man at all.
Your existence has to honor your Creator.

*Praise ye the Lord . I will praise the Lord with
my whole heart, in the assembly of the upright,
and in the congregation.*
Psalm 111:1

*And the rib, which the Lord God had taken
from man, made he a woman, and brought her
unto the man. And Adam said,* **This is now
bone of my bones, and flesh of my flesh:**
*she shall be called Woman, because she was
taken out of Man. Therefore shall a man leave
his father and his mother, and shall cleave unto
his wife: and they shall* **be one** *flesh.*
Genesis 2:22-24

In the beginning, God only had one name for
both; he called both man and woman Adam. It
was a name of authority; it represented the
image and likeness of God. However, after
Adam missed his appointment with God and
blamed it on the woman, the name Eve began

to appear, marking the division in the Garden. **God was not disappointed by the sin of Adam, but he was disappointed when Adam missed his appointed time with Him. God removed man and woman from the garden because they were divided. Thus the woman was left to be called "Eve" all alone without her counterpart, her teacher, and her protector.**

The garden is a Godly Kingdom. Marriage is from God's Kingdom. God finds no honor in division. So, if the kingdom is divided, it would have to be restored. Everything that's lacking in the world has to do with the division of man from himself.

But seek ye first the kingdom of God, and his righteousness; and all these things shall be added unto you.
Matthew 6:33

Everyone knows when something is missing, especially if that something is half of you. Some people have turned to drugs; others have become alcoholics and destroyed their own lives. All of the self-destruction that we see today is an effort of man to fill a gap. What gap? Some call her "Eve", others called her a "woman." These "names" are nothing but an attempt to devalue and individualize a unit of a supreme being God called Adam (man). I am convinced that the primary message of the Kingdom is for man to reconcile with self and to show himself whole in the presence (garden) of God.

So, if man has looked for the Kingdom (righteousness, peace, prosperity and joy), but has not found it, it is because man has not reconciled with self (found a wife).

CHAPTER 7

Pursue Your Wife & Restore Your Marriage

First and foremost, the woman in your head doesn't exist; that's why you've never met her. You have created a picture based on falsehoods or testimonials that have led you to put a set of expectations on yourself that isn't achievable. So, you have gotten married to a woman (yourself). Being just like you (led by lies or testimonials), your other half has measured herself using the standards of what she has seen on television and via social media; she has done this in order to capture herself (you). Two years have passed and things are changing, but no one has prepared you for the sixty pounds she has gained over the holidays and the back injury she received at a volleyball tournament last summer. So, you looked around to find yourself (your woman), but what you saw was a sixty-pound heavier version of yourself (your wife) limping around the house. Reality has become an offense because it has ruined your plans to accomplish an unrealistic goal.

So ought men to love their wives as their own bodies. He that loveth his wife loveth himself. For no man ever yet hated his own flesh; but nourisheth and cherisheth it, even as the Lord the church: For we are members of his body, of his flesh, and of his bones.
Ephesians 5:28-30

You are not crazy!

For as he thinketh in his heart, so is he: Eat and drink, saith he to thee; but his heart is not with thee.
Proverbs 23:7

The reason why the woman in your head doesn't exist is because you have to create her. In the age of high speed internet, fast cars, and fast food, man thinks that finding a wife is like flipping a light switch. Next time you think about that woman in your head, take a selfie and look at it. If you don't like what you see, you've got more work to do.

Whoso findeth a wife findeth a good thing, and obtaineth favor of the Lord.
Proverbs 18:22

Second of all, marriage is something sacred that was created by God in order to cultivate a kingdom. Don't be among the unlearned who deflowered this sacred union through ungodly legislation or propaganda.

And God blessed them, and God said unto them, Be fruitful, and multiply, and replenish the earth, and subdue it: and have dominion over the fish of the sea, and over the fowl of the air, and over every living thing that moveth upon the earth.
Genesis 1:28

Here is a scripture that speaks about guarding your marriage in a very profound way. Jesus referred to the church as His bride. So, Apostle Paul uses the relationship that Jesus has established with His church to teach the Ephesians about marriage. Let's take a look... *Ephesians 5:1-33 says:* ***... Be ye therefore followers of God, as dear children; And walk in love, as Christ also hath loved us, and hath given himself for us an offering and a sacrifice to God for a sweet smelling savour.*** A husband must love his wife like Jesus loves the church and gave Himself for her. ***But fornication, and all uncleanness, or covetousness, let it not be once named among you, as becometh saints; Neither filthiness, nor foolish talking, nor jesting, which are not convenient: but rather giving of thanks. For this ye know, that no whoremonger, nor unclean person, nor covetous man, who is an idolater, hath any inheritance in the kingdom of Christ and of God.*** In verses 3 and 4, Apostle Paul noted that, not only should we avoid these things, but we shouldn't even allow them to be rumored among us. ***Let no man deceive you with vain words: for because of these things cometh*** *the wrath of God upon the children of disobedience. Be not ye therefore partakers with them. For ye were sometimes darkness, but now are ye light in the Lord: walk as children of light: (For the fruit of the Spirit is in all goodness and righteousness and truth;) Proving what is acceptable unto the Lord.* In verses 6-10, he is advising us not to participate in filthiness. Furthermore, in verse 6, he warned them about ungodly counsel. *And have no fellowship with the unfruitful works of darkness, but rather reprove them.* Apostle Paul repeated that we should not be anywhere where filthiness is being practiced. *For it is a shame even to speak of those things which are done of them in secret. But all things that are reproved are made manifest by the light: for whatsoever doth make manifest is light. Wherefore he saith, Awake thou that sleepest, and arise from the dead, and Christ shall give thee light. See then that ye walk circumspectly, not as fools, but as wise, Redeeming the time, because the days are evil. Wherefore be ye not unwise, but understanding what the will of the Lord is. And be not drunk with wine, wherein is excess; but be filled with the Spirit; Speaking to yourselves in psalms and hymns and spiritual songs, singing and making melody in your heart to the Lord;* Speaking in a pleasant tone. *Giving thanks always for all things unto God and the Father in the name of our Lord Jesus Christ;* carrying of a spirit of thanks giving *Submitting yourselves one to another in the fear of God.* This spirit of submission is NOT the same as having low self-esteem; it means to submit in love. *Wives, submit yourselves unto your own husbands, as unto the Lord. For the husband is the head of the wife, even as Christ is the head of the church: and he is the saviour of the body.* Apostle Paul gave a brief reminder that he is using Christ as a role model for this teaching. *Therefore as the church is subject unto Christ, so let the wives be to their own husbands in everything. Husbands, love your wives, even as Christ also loved the church, and gave himself for it;* a man sacrifices himself for his wife. *That he might sanctify and cleanse it with the washing of water by the word, That he might present it to himself a glorious church, not having spot, or wrinkle, or any such thing; but that it should be holy and without blemish.* Apostle Paul spoke about preparing your wife by teaching her in love, removing all wrinkles, spots and blemishes, and then, presenting her to yourself as a glorious wife. *So ought men to love their wives as their own bodies. He that loveth his wife loveth himself. For no man ever yet hated his own flesh; but nourisheth and cherisheth it, even as the Lord the church:* He was teaching about being a protector and provider for her. *For we are members of his body, of his flesh, and of his bones. For this cause shall a man leave his father and mother, and shall be joined unto his wife, and they two shall be one flesh. This is a great mystery: but I speak concerning Christ and the church. Nevertheless let every one of you in particular so love his wife even as himself; and the wife see that she reverence her*

husband. Apostle Paul referred to the knowledge of the relationship between Jesus and the church as a mystery. You have to want this knowledge in other to dig for it.

CHAPTER 8

Unforgiveness and a Covenant Relationship

The Danger of Unforgiveness

Unforgiveness is holding onto pain and refusing to let go. There are five reasons for unforgiveness:

1. Pride
2. Selfishness
3. Arrogance
4. Lack of knowledge
5. Sign of weakness

Unforgiveness is the number one poison that's eating up families today. It is a sin because if you cannot forgive, how can you love? It is not just a sin, it is an iniquity. *Do not let your yesterday stop you from enjoying your today and rob you of your tomorrow.*

11 Facts About Unforgiveness

1. Unforgiveness reveals that we don't really love Jesus.

This is my commandment, That ye love one another, as I have loved you.
John 15:12

2. Unforgiveness prevents God from forgiving our sins.

But if ye forgive not men their trespasses, neither will your Father forgive your trespasses. Matthew 6:15
And when ye stand praying, forgive, if ye have ought against any: that your Father also which is in heaven may forgive you your trespasses. Mark 11:25-26

3. Unforgiveness opens us up to the enemy.

Then came Peter to him, and said, Lord, how oft shall my brother sin against me, and I forgive him? till seven times? Jesus saith unto him, I say not unto thee, Until seven times: but, Until seventy times seven.

Matthew 18:21-22

4. Unforgiveness can be traced to traumatic life experiences, low self-esteem, and lack of faith.

5. Unforgiveness limits us from achieving the abundant life that God has promised us.

6. Unforgiveness is a weapon in the hands of the enemy.
To whom ye forgive anything, I forgive also: for if I forgave anything, to whom I forgave it, for your sakes forgave I it in the person of Christ; Lest Satan should get an advantage of us: for we are not ignorant of his devices.
2 Corinthians 2:10-11

7. Unforgiveness hinders our prayers.
Therefore I say unto you, What things soever ye desire, when ye pray, believe that ye receive them, and ye shall have them. And when ye stand praying, forgive, if ye have ought against any: that your Father also which

is in heaven may forgive you your trespasses.
Mark 11:24-25

8. Unforgiveness hinders our faith.

9. Unforgiveness can defile a person.
Looking diligently lest any man fail of the grace of God; lest any root of bitterness springing up trouble you, and thereby many be defiled;
Hebrew 12:15

10. Unforgiveness can prevent us from being spiritually fruitful.
I am the vine, ye are the branches: He that abideth in me, and I in him, the same bringeth forth much fruit: for without me ye can do nothing.
John 15:5

11. Unforgiveness can make you miss heaven.
We know that we have passed from death unto life, because we love the brethren. He that loveth not his brother abideth in death.
1 John 3:14

You will not embrace what's ahead of you if you can't forgive what's behind you.

Overcoming the Three Major Seeds of Temptation in Your Marriage

1. **The seed of doubt**

   Now the serpent was more subtil than any beast of the field which the Lord God had made. And he said unto the woman, Yea, hath God said, Ye shall not eat of every tree of the garden?
   Genesis 3:1

2. **The seed of deceit**

   And the serpent said unto the woman, Ye shall not surely die: For God doth know that in the day ye eat thereof, then your eyes shall be opened, and ye shall be as gods, knowing good and evil.
   Genesis 3:4-5

3. **The seed of desire**

   And when the woman saw that the tree was good for food, and that it was pleasant to the eyes, and a tree to be desired to make one wise, she took of the fruit thereof, and did eat, and gave also unto her husband with her; and he did eat.

Genesis 3:6

Likewise, ye husbands, dwell with them according to knowledge, giving honour unto the wife, as unto the weaker vessel, and as being heirs together of the grace of life; that your prayers be not hindered.
1 Peter 3:7

That the sons of God saw the daughters of men that they were fair; and they took them wives of all which they chose. And the Lord said, My spirit shall not always strive with man, for that he also is flesh: yet his days shall be a hundred and twenty years.
Genesis 6:2-3

Conquering and Overcoming the Desires of the Flesh and Taking Control

All of our earthly desires are from the flesh. So, if we desire the things from heaven, we have to crucify the flesh and live by the Spirit of God. In **Galatians 5:24-26,** Apostle Paul says: *And they that are Christ's have crucified the flesh with the affections and lusts. If we live in the Spirit, let us also walk in the Spirit. Let us not be desirous of vain glory, provoking one another, envying one another.* When we are afflicted, it is often because the flesh has exhausted its boundaries. Heart attacks, diabetes, depression, and hypertension, just to name a few, are all affairs of the flesh. I encourage you to be filled with the Spirit of God so you can overcome the cunning craftiness of the enemy.

It is the spirit that quickeneth; the flesh profiteth nothing: the words that I speak unto you, they are spirit, and they are life.
John 6:63

Watch and pray, that ye enter not into temptation: the spirit indeed is willing, but the flesh is weak.
Matthew 26:41

And you, being dead in your sins and the uncircumcision of your flesh, hath he quickened together with him, having forgiven you all trespasses; blotting out the handwriting of ordinances that was against us, which was contrary to us, and took it out of the way, nailing it to his cross; And having spoiled principalities and powers, he made a shew of them openly, triumphing over them in it.
Colossians 2:13-15

This I say then, Walk in the Spirit, and ye shall not fulfil the lust of the flesh.
Galatians 5:16

And hope maketh not ashamed; because the love of God is shed abroad in our hearts by the Holy Ghost which is given unto us.
Romans 5:5

The Building of a Covenant Relationship

A covenant relationship is a pledge that two people have mutually made to one another regarding their relationship; relationships have an acquired anticipated reward. God's covenant relationship with Israel was a promise. It is the same promise He has extended to the Gentiles; that's you. *And he spake unto the children of Israel, saying, When your children shall ask their fathers in time to come, saying, What mean these stones? Then ye shall let your children know, saying, Israel came over this Jordan on dry land. For the Lord your God dried up the waters of Jordan from before you, until ye were passed over, as the Lord your God did to the Red sea, which he dried up from before us, until we were gone over: Joshua 4:21-23*

Intimacy leaves no room for secrets. Secret relationships lead to secret places. The secret places lead to secret battles, and when we get to secret places, we start drawing secret honey. (Refer to the story of Samson and

Delilah in Judges 16:4-31). You cannot have a healthy relationship without trust. Trust is the bedrock of intimacy.

Restoring Intimacy With Your Wife

A husband's absenteeism starves his marriage. As a result, he gives outdated resources to his marriage, not what it currently needs. God gave Abraham a word to climb up the mountain and sacrifice Isaac, but when he got on top of the mountain, there was a new word waiting for him. Intimacy gives ear to the needs of the relationship. The same is true for marital intimacy.

When a husband struggles, he tries to give to God what he ought to give to his marriage. So, he will try to be super-spiritual in his attempt to solve a natural issue.
Note: God will not come down from His Holy place, nor will He send an angel to do for you what He has already equipped you to do for yourself.

Fear is the enemy of faith. If you have done something wrong and are wondering if you can fix that mess you have created, yes you can. Sometimes, we are afraid of the mess, but God knows well how to turn a mess into a message. (Look at the story of creation). God took mess, He formed mess, and put His mouth on the mess. The Bible says that He breathed life into **mess**, and then said that He'd formed **mess** in His own image—the image of perfection. It doesn't matter how bad your mess is, God can breathe life into it. Don't give up on your marriage, regardless of how messy it is.

And I will restore to you the years that the locust hath eaten, the cankerworm, and the caterpiller, and the palmerworm, my great army which I sent among you.
Joel 2:25

Jesus spoke also the parable of the fig tree that wasn't producing any fruit …
A certain man had a fig tree planted in his vineyard; and he came and sought fruit thereon, and found none. Then said he unto

the dresser of his vineyard, Behold, these three years I come seeking fruit on this fig tree, and find none: cut it down; why cumbereth it the ground? And he answering said unto him, Lord, let it alone this year also, till I shall dig about it, and dung it.
Luke 13:6

Your wife is your fruit tree and you are the dresser of the vineyard. You are responsible for removing any bad weeds that are around her. You have got to let go of some friends and remove yourself from among certain people in order for you both to survive. The problem in the marriage is often not the two people, it is the weeds around them. You have got to do some digging around your marriage. That girlfriend has to go. You have to remove your parents away from your marriage.

Three Principles of a Covenant Relationship

To have a relationship, it requires a second person. The covenant relationship will be gagged by reciprocity. Once established, you now have a covenant partner secured by intimacy.

Too much + too soon = disaster

Elisha and Elijah Built a Covenant Relationship in Three Places

1. Gilgal is a place of cutting (circumcision). In other words, you have to remove every impure thing out of your relationship. Some friends are necessary, but others ought to be removed far away. Regardless of whether it is your relationship with God or your marriage with your spouse, in order for that relationship to survive, you have to do some cutting. No plant grows with bad weeds around it.

2. Bethel is a place of prayer. Covenant partners are built through prayer. You may have been through hardships, and sometimes, you worship and pray to keep from crying. But what you have grown to become will keep you together.

3. Jericho is the fortified city. The city with walls. Relationships can't be created or maintained from behind the walls. In order to have a covenant relationship, you have to take down the insecurities.

The Five Characteristics of a Covenant Partner

1. They can handle change. A covenant partner is a tomorrow partner.
2. Covenant partners don't run away.
3. A covenant partner trusts God. A covenant partner says, "I will trust God for you. When you can't carry it, I will carry it for you. When you don't have faith, I will have faith for you."
4. A covenant partner trusts himself.
5. A covenant partner is not a project.

CHAPTER 9

Marriage & Sex

Solo Scriptura

Marriage: man and woman

Therefore shall a man leave his father and his mother, and shall cleave unto his wife: and they shall be one flesh.
Genesis 2:24

Now concerning the things whereof ye wrote unto me: It is good for a man not to touch a woman. Nevertheless, to avoid fornication, let every man have his own wife, and let every woman have her own husband. Let the husband render unto the wife due benevolence: and likewise also the wife unto the husband. The wife hath not power of her own body, but the husband: and likewise also

the husband hath not power of his own body, but the wife.
1 Corinthians 7:1-4

And he answered and said unto them, Have ye not read, that he which made them at the beginning made them male and female, And said, For this cause shall a man leave father and mother, and shall cleave to his wife: and they twain shall be one flesh? Wherefore they are no more twain, but one flesh. What therefore God hath joined together, let not man put asunder.
Matthew 19:4-6

Homosexuality
Sex: Man with man

And thou shalt not let any of thy seed pass through the fire to Molech, neither shalt thou profane the name of thy God: I am the Lord. Thou shalt not lie with mankind, as with womankind: it is abomination.
Leviticus 18:21-22

If a man also lie with mankind, as he lieth with a woman, both of them have committed an abomination: they shall surely be put to death; their blood shall be upon them.
Leviticus 20:13

Bestiality
Sex with animals

Neither shalt thou lie with any beast to defile thyself therewith: neither shall any woman stand before a beast to lie down thereto: it is confusion. Defile not ye yourselves in any of these things: for in all these the nations are defiled which I cast out before you: And the land is defiled: therefore I do visit the iniquity thereof upon it, and the land itself vomiteth out her inhabitants.
Leviticus 18:23-25

And if a man lie with a beast, he shall surely be put to death: and ye shall slay the beast. And if a woman approach unto any beast, and lie down thereto, thou shalt kill the woman, and the beast: they shall surely be put to death;

their blood shall be upon them.
Leviticus 20:15-16

For this cause God gave them up unto vile
affections: for even their women did change
the natural use into that which is against
nature: And likewise also the men, leaving the
natural use of the woman, burned in their lust
one toward another; men with men working
that which is unseemly, and receiving in
themselves that recompence of their error
which was meet. And even as they did not like
to retain God in their knowledge, God gave
them over to a reprobate mind, to do those
things which are not convenient;
Romans 1:26-28

Know ye not that the unrighteous shall not
inherit the kingdom of God? Be not deceived:
neither fornicators, nor idolaters, nor
adulterers, nor effeminate, nor abusers of
themselves with mankind, Nor thieves, nor
covetous, nor drunkards, nor revilers, nor
extortioners, shall inherit the kingdom of God.
And such were some of you: but ye are

washed, but ye are sanctified, but ye are justified in the name of the Lord Jesus, and by the Spirit of our God. All things are lawful unto me, but all things are not expedient: all things are lawful for me, but I will not be brought under the power of any.
1 Corinthians 6:9-12

But we know that the law is good, if a man use it lawfully; Knowing this, that the law is not made for a righteous man, but for the lawless and disobedient, for the ungodly and for sinners, for unholy and profane, for murderers of fathers and murderers of mothers, for manslayers, For whoremongers, for them that defile themselves with mankind, for menstealers, for liars, for perjured persons, and if there be any other thing that is contrary to sound doctrine;
1 Timothy 1:8-10

CHAPTER 10

The Desires & Priorities of a Man

The Five Secrets of a Man of Destiny

1. The Ability to Prioritize

But seek ye first the kingdom of God, and his righteousness;and all these things shall be added unto you.
Matthew 6:33

A) The Kingdom Priority

But seek ye first the kingdom of God, and his righteousness;and all these things shall be added unto you.
Matthew 6:33

God first, **Family** and **Church**

- To seek = is to pursue
- First = above everything else
- Kingdom = the object of your pursuit

—God

Kingdom Focus - In a kingdom, it is in the best interest of the king for every citizen to be well. A kingdom is evaluated based on the well-being of its citizens. Commonwealth is the common economy of kingdom. Jesus said:
And as ye go, preach, saying, The kingdom of heaven is at hand. Heal the sick, cleanse the lepers, raise the dead, cast out devils: freely ye have received, freely give.
Matthew 10:7-8

B) **Family Priority**
- Be careful who you bring to your family.
- Purposes trump profit—money is an essential thing, but it is not everything.
- Pray over the process of becoming the product that God wants you to be.
- Don't limit God down to your choices.

If you have been rejected and accused, stay courageous. The stone that was rejected has become the chief cornerstone.
*If you have never been rejected, you cannot

be selected.

*You were built for the adversity; it only made you stronger.

*You are God's crazy choice – He called you.

C) **Church Priority**

Look for opportunities to commune with the brethren. Together, you are stronger than when you are alone.

*Not forsaking the assembling of ourselves together, as the manner of some is; but exhorting one another: and so much the more, as ye see the day approaching.
Hebrews 10:25*

*Go ye therefore, and teach all nations, baptizing them in the name of the Father, and of the Son, and of the Holy Ghost.
Matthew 28:19*

And the things that thou hast heard of me among many witnesses, the same commit thou to faithful men, who shall be able to teach others also.

2 Timothy 2:2

2. Master the Art of Responsibility
If ye be willing and obedient, ye shall eat the good of the land: But if ye refuse and rebel, ye shall be devoured with the sword: for the mouth of the Lord hath spoken it.
Isaiah 1:19-20

Keep therefore the words of this covenant, and do them, that ye may prosper in all that ye do.
Deuteronomy 29:9

The Lord is good, a stronghold in the day of trouble; and he knoweth them that trust in him.
Nahum 1:7

The voice of joy, and the voice of gladness, the voice of the bridegroom, and the voice of the bride, the voice of them that shall say, Praise the Lord of hosts: for the Lord is good; for his mercy endureth forever.
Jeremiah 33:11

Praise the Lord; for the Lord is good: sing

praises unto his name; for it is pleasant.
Psalm 135:3

O taste and see that the Lord is good: blessed is the man that trusteth in him.
Psalm 34:8

3. Nurture Your Vision
And be renewed in the spirit of your mind.
Ephesians 4:23

For as he thinketh in his heart, so is he: Eat and drink, saith he to thee; but his heart is not with thee.
Proverbs 23:7

4. Commit to Your Dreams. David took a stone; Samson took a jawbone.

Arise, shine; for thy light is come, and the glory of the Lord is risen upon thee.
Isaiah 60:1

*The opportunities you capture will fulfill your purpose on earth.

5. Master the Ability to Focus.

Apostle Paul said, "My heart is fixed, oh God. My heart is fixed."

Man's failure is not because of the devil, it is his broken focus.

O God, my heart is fixed; I will sing and give praise, even with my glory.
Psalm 108:1

For we are the circumcision, which worship God in the spirit, and rejoice in Christ Jesus, and have no confidence in the flesh.
Philippians 3:3

For the flesh lusteth against the Spirit, and the Spirit against the flesh: and these are contrary the one to the other: so that ye cannot do the things that ye would.
Galatians 5:17

The law of focus:
What you focus on will determine whether you fail or succeed. The first law God gave to

Adam was about his focus. Philippians 3:13-14, Lamentation 3:51, Psalm 101:3. Your focus decides where you excel. Below are a few ways to master your focus:

1. Keep a Master To-Do List at All Times. Write it down—One unbeliever who's focused will do more than a believer who is not focused. Your mind is for creativity, not storage. Your mind is like a garden where you plant flowers, pull weeds and kill snakes. God gave you a mind to pre-play your future.

2. Planning—When you schedule an appointment, plan the focus of the appointment. Everything is competing for your focus. Every problem in marriage, work or ministry can be traced to a loss of focus.

The Five Desires of a Man after God's Own Heart

1. A desire to be filled with the Spirit of God
And they were all filled with the Holy Ghost, and began to speak with other tongues, as the Spirit gave them utterance.
Acts 4:4

And be not drunk with wine, wherein is excess; but be filled with the Spirit; Speaking to yourselves in psalms and hymns and spiritual songs, singing and making melody in your heart to the Lord.
Ephesians 5:18-19

And it shall come to pass afterward, that I will pour out my spirit upon all flesh; and your sons and your daughters shall prophesy, your old men shall dream dreams, your young men shall see visions.
Joel 2:28

2. True worshipper

But the hour cometh, and now is, when the true worshippers shall worship the Father in spirit and in truth: for the Father seeketh such to worship him. God is a Spirit: and they that worship him must worship him in spirit and in truth.
John 4:23-24

3. A student's heart towards the things of God

For this cause we also, since the day we heard it, do not cease to pray for you, and to desire that ye might be filled with the knowledge of his will in all wisdom and spiritual understanding.
Colossians 1:9

And to know the love of Christ, which passeth knowledge, that ye might be filled with all the fullness of God.
Ephesians 3:19

Wisdom is the principal thing; therefore get wisdom: and with all thy getting get understanding. Proverbs 4:7

The fear of the Lord is the beginning of wisdom: a good understanding have all they that do his commandments: his praise endureth for ever.
Psalms 111:10

For the earth shall be filled with the knowledge of the glory of the Lord, as the waters cover the sea.
Habakkuk 2:14

Study to shew thyself approved unto God, a workman that needeth not to be ashamed, rightly dividing the word of truth.
2 Timothy 2:15

4. A desire to be pastored and counseled
And I will give you pastors according to mine heart, which shall feed you with knowledge and understanding.
Jeremiah 3:15

And he gave some, apostles; and some, prophets; and some, evangelists; and some, pastors and teachers; For the perfecting of the saints, for the work of the ministry, for the edifying of the body of Christ: till we all come in the unity of the faith, and of the knowledge of the Son of God, unto a perfect man, unto the measure of the stature of the fulness of Christ: That we henceforth be no more children, tossed to and fro, and carried about with every wind of doctrine, by the sleight of men, and cunning craftiness, whereby they lie in wait to deceive; But speaking the truth in love, may grow up into him in all things, which is the

head, even Christ.
Ephesians 4:11-15

5. A desire to commune with one another

And when he had given thanks, he brake it,
and said, Take, eat: this is my body, which is
broken for you: this do in remembrance of me.
1 Corinthians 11:24

CHAPTER 11

Understanding and Overcoming Discouragement

Four Weapons the Enemy Uses to Discourage a Man

1. Delays, setbacks, unmet expectations

Then said he unto me, Fear not, Daniel: for from the first day that thou didst set thine heart to understand, and to chasten thyself before thy God, thy words were heard, and I am come for thy words.
But the prince of the kingdom of Persia withstood me one and twenty days: but, lo, Michael, one of the chief princes, came to help me; and I remained there with the kings of Persia. Daniel 10:12-13

2. Deception-every failure in your life can be traced to a place of deceit.

One who listens to ungodly counsel will continuously make ungodly decisions that eventually destroy marriages and lives. Any decision that does not glorify God is ungodly. *And the devil that deceived them was cast into the lake of fire and brimstone, where the beast and the false prophet are, and shall be tormented day and night for ever and ever. Revelation 20:10*

3. Distraction—something that redirect your focus.

And the cares of this world, and the deceitfulness of riches, and the lusts of other things entering in, choke the word, and it becometh unfruitful. Mark 4:19

4. Disappointment—displeasure caused by unmet expectation

But think on me when it shall be well with thee, and shew kindness, I pray thee, unto me, and make mention of me unto Pharaoh, and bring me out of this house:
For indeed I was stolen away out of the land of

the Hebrews: and here also have I done nothing that they should put me into the dungeon. When the chief baker saw that the interpretation was good, he said unto Joseph, I also was in my dream, and, behold, I had three white baskets on my head:

And in the uppermost basket there was of all manner of bakemeats for Pharaoh; and the birds did eat them out of the basket upon my head. And Joseph answered and said, This is the interpretation thereof: The three baskets are three days:

Yet within three days shall Pharaoh lift up thy head from off thee, and shall hang thee on a tree; and the birds shall eat thy flesh from off thee. And it came to pass the third day, which was Pharaoh's birthday, that he made a feast unto all his servants: and he lifted up the head of the chief butler and of the chief baker among his servants. And he restored the chief butler unto his butlership again; and he gave the cup into Pharaoh's hand: But he hanged the chief baker: as Joseph had interpreted to them. Yet did not the chief butler remember Joseph, but forgat him. Genesis 40:14-23

Seven Ways to Overcome Discouragement

Recommended Reading
1 Samuel 21:1-15

1. Re-examine your faith.

2. Evaluate your current influence.
   A) Who is talking to me? What am I watching on television?
   B) What words am I listening to? Words decide feelings and focus.
   C) How far can you go? The Devil wants you to give up and wear you out.

And he shall speak great words against the most High, and shall wear out the saints of the most High, and think to change times and laws: and they shall be given into his hand until a time and times and the dividing of time.
Daniel 7:25

3. What has become my dominant focus?

4. Invest in listening and reading what other men have overcome.

For a just man falleth seven times, and riseth up again: but the wicked shall fall into mischief. Proverbs 24:16

5. Remind yourself that feelings are fleeting.
   A) Focus creates feelings.
   B) Feelings are not facts; they can be changed. Even the most powerful man gets discouraged at some point in his life.

6. Review your success.
   A) David visited the camp of the enemy because he was discouraged.

7. Seek to self-motivate.
   A. Discouragement is for a season.
   B. Focus decides longevity.
   C. Replace discouragement with the picture of tomorrow.
   D. No man can break you out of discouragement but yourself.

There are Three Things a Man Must Never Do

1. Never burden your children with whatever it is that's discouraging you, spiritual or biological.
2. Never seek wisdom from the unlearned.
3. Never seek counseling from someone who has not overcome anything.

Encourage yourself - David says: "I encourage myself in the Lord."

Change your atmosphere - Change who and what you are listening to, doing, or watching.

Learn from the situation - Great leaders come out of bad times.

Never repeat the mistake - The more we are afflicted, the more we grow.

Build stamina from what you've been through - I am a radical sinner, so when I pray, I pray radically.

Out of adversities come power and strength. Out of sickness come a prayer warrior.

CHAPTER 12

The Power of Intimacy

The Power of (into-me-see)

*Therefore I write these things being absent,
lest being present I should use sharpness,
according to the power which the Lord hath
given me to edification, and not to destruction.
Finally, brethren, farewell. Be perfect, be of
good comfort, be of one mind, live in peace;
and the God of love and peace shall be with
you. Greet one another with an holy kiss. All
the saints salute you.*
2 Corinthians 13:10-13

The Ten Mile Road to Intimacy

1. Listen without interrupting.
*A fool hath no delight in understanding, but that
his heart may discover itself.*

Proverbs 18:2

2. Speak without accusing.

Wherefore, my beloved brethren, let every man be swift to hear, slow to speak, slow to wrath.
James 1:19

3. Give without sparing.

He coveteth greedily all the day long: but the righteous giveth and spareth not.
Proverbs 21:26

4. Pray without ceasing.

For this cause we also, since the day we heard it, do not cease to pray for you, and to desire that ye might be filled with the knowledge of his will in all wisdom and spiritual understanding;
Colossians 1:9

5. Answer without arguing.

Better is a dry morsel, and quietness therewith, than an house full of sacrifices with strife.
Proverbs 17:1

6. Share without pretending.

*But speaking the truth in love, may grow up
into him in all things, which is the head, even
Christ.*
Ephesians 4:15

7. Enjoy without complaining.

*Do all things without murmurings and
disputings.*
Philippians 2:14

8. Believe without wavering.

*Beareth all things, believeth all things, hopeth
all things, endureth all things.*
1 Corinthians 13:7

9. Forgive without punishing.

*Forbearing one another, and forgiving one
another, if any man have a quarrel against any:
even as Christ forgave you, so also do ye.*
Colossians 3:13

10. Be in love

*A new commandment I give unto you, That ye
love one another; as I have loved you, that ye
also love one another. By this shall all men*

*know that ye are my disciples, if ye have love
one to another.*
John 13:34-35

Intimacy with God

*And it came to pass, as she continued praying
before the Lord, that Eli marked her mouth.
Now Hannah, she spake in her heart; only her
lips moved, but her voice was not heard:
therefore Eli thought she had been drunken.
And Eli said unto her, How long wilt thou be
drunken? put away thy wine from thee. And
Hannah answered and said, No, my lord, I am
a woman of a sorrowful spirit: I have drunk
neither wine nor strong drink, but have poured
out my soul before the Lord. Count not thine
handmaid for a daughter of Belial: for out of the
abundance of my complaint and grief have I
spoken hitherto. Then Eli answered and said,
Go in peace: and the God of Israel grant thee
thy petition that thou hast asked of him. And
she said, Let thine handmaid find grace in thy
sight. So the woman went her way, and did
eat, and her countenance was no more sad.*

1 Samuel 1:12-18

Intercession: the action of intervening on behalf of another.

Likewise the Spirit also helpeth our infirmities: for we know not what we should pray for as we ought: but the Spirit itself maketh intercession for us with groanings which cannot be uttered.
Romans 8:26

Wherefore he is able also to save them to the uttermost that come unto God by him, seeing he ever liveth to make intercession for them.
Hebrews 7:25

Lamentation: the passionate expression of grief or sorrow; weeping.
And Jeremiah lamented for Josiah: and all the singing men and the singing women spake of Josiah in their lamentations to this day, and made them an ordinance in Israel: and, behold, they are written in the lamentations.
2 Chronicles 35:25

Petition Prayer: The action of bringing forth a request to God in prayer on behalf of another.
For this child I prayed; and the Lord hath given me my petition which I asked of him.
1 Samuel 1:27

We will rejoice in thy salvation, and in the name of our God we will set up our banners: the Lord fulfill all thy petitions.
Psalm 20:5

And if we know that he hear us, whatsoever we ask, we know that we have the petitions that we desired of him.
1 John 5:15

Supplication: the action of asking or begging for something earnestly or humbly.
I exhort therefore, that, first of all, supplications, prayers, intercessions, and giving of thanks, be made for all men;
1 Timothy 2:1

Communion prayer: There, your spirit prays. Your conversation with God continues anywhere because He is with you.

Things to Remember When You Pray

- Prayer is dialogue.
- You're requesting something from God.
- Petition to God.
- Set times to pray.
- Don't be afraid to pray.
- Speak to God like you do to a person.
- Decide your reason for praying.
- Prayer will get you closer to God.
- Acknowledge God for who He is to you.
- Clear your mind so you can focus on God.
- Use God's own Word and promises when praying.

The Lord's Prayer

Though you may have been taught that this is the Lord's Prayer, but in truth, this is the disciples' prayer. The Lord's Prayer can be found in the Garden of Gethsemane. This prayer was given by Jesus to serve as a blueprint on how to approach God:

After this manner therefore pray ye: Our Father which art in heaven, Hallowed be thy name. **This is to magnify the Name of Jesus when praying.** *Thy kingdom come.* **This is to call, acknowledge and submit to God's Kingdom.** *Thy will be done in earth, as it is in heaven.* **This teaches us how to submit to the will of God and place it above our own will.** *Give us this day our daily bread.* **This is show dependency on God alone.** *And forgive us our debts, as we forgive our debtors.* **This is where you ask God to forgive your sins. This passage is also confirmation regarding a previous scripture where Jesus said to forgive others so that God can forgive you.** *And lead us not into temptation, but deliver us from evil:* **God doesn't lead us into temptation; when we submit to His Will, He makes our paths straight.** *For thine is the kingdom, and the power, and the glory, forever.* **This is an example of how to close every prayer, both in worship and in praise.** *Amen.* **When you close with an "Amen," you acknowledge His Will one more time by**

saying, "So be it" *(Matthew 6:9-13).*

God is an on-time God.
Sometimes, when we think God is not
answering our prayers, we are given an
opportunity to submit ourselves in worship
while waiting for our desired answers. We often
misunderstood that the time between the
prayer and the answer is a time for worship
and praise, celebrating the anticipated answer.

Then Job arose, and rent his mantle, and
shaved his head, and fell down upon the
ground, and worshipped.
Job 1:20

Contrast: worship and praise
In times of trials, it is the most difficult to
worship. Martha and Mary, sisters of Lazarus,
found it difficult because they thought Jesus
had not heard about their trouble. But their
answer was in their worship.

Then when Mary was come where Jesus was,
and saw him, she fell down at his feet, saying

unto him, Lord, if thou hadst been here, my
brother had not died.
John 11:32

A life of praise, an attitude of worship and a
daily relationship with the Word through
devotion and prayer will bring you into intimacy
with God. When you have built the foundation
of faith, you have built a bedrock for intimacy.
You will make mistakes, but don't let shame
and guilt stop you from achieving greatness
because it is through your hardships and
overcomings that you will acquire wisdom.
Many great men who have risen to
phenomenal heights in leadership have
survived some of the harshest trials. The more
we are afflicted, the more we grow.
Remember, to ask God for forgiveness and
return to worship immediately. As bad you may
sin, when you pray, pray and worship radically.
Give yourself to God without reservation. After
all, what have you got to lose? Power and
strength come from adversity. Out of sickness
comes a prayer warrior on fire for God.

CHAPTER 13

The Man Who Prays

But they that wait upon the Lord shall renew their strength; they shall mount up with wings as eagles; they shall run, and not be weary; and they shall walk, and not faint.
Isaiah 40:31

30 Daily Devotional Prayers That Will Renew Your Spirit

Day # 1
Pray to be Faithful

Moreover it is required in stewards that one be found faithful.
1 Corinthians 4:2

Most of us know what a fair-weather fan is: the team supporter who supports the team only under one condition—the team maintains a winning record. If the team is on a losing streak, the fair-weather fan will likely stay home. The opposite of a fair-weather fan is a faithful fan.

The biblical equivalent of a faithful fan is a steward—one who has been anointed and commissioned to carry out a specific task. And the chief characteristic of a steward is faithfulness *(1 Corinthians 4:2)*.

The steward will carry out his or her commission regardless of the cost. The Bible speaks often of stewards: Joseph in Egypt, the faithful steward in Jesus' parables, church overseers, and the apostle Paul—a steward of the grace of God. In every case, faithfulness was the chief requirement. We might ask ourselves whether we are a fair-weather or a faithful fan of God's assignments for our lives. How inconvenienced are we willing to be for the sake of the Gospel?

God has made every born again Christian a

steward of the gift of salvation by grace, a gift we are to use for His glory. Let's pray today to be faithful stewards.

And Joseph was brought down to Egypt; and Potiphar, an officer of Pharaoh, captain of the guard, an Egyptian, bought him of the hands of the Ishmeelites, which had brought him down thither. And the LORD was with Joseph, and he was a prosperous man; and he was in the house of his master the Egyptian. And his master saw that the LORD was with him, and that the LORD made all that he did to prosper in his hand. And Joseph found grace in his sight, and he served him: and he made him overseer over his house, and all that he had he put into his hand. And it came to pass from the time that he had made him overseer in his house, and over all that he had, that the LORD blessed the Egyptian's house for Joseph's sake; and the blessing of the LORD was upon all that he had in the house, and in the field. And he left all that he had in Joseph's hand; and he knew not ought he had, save the bread which he did eat. And Joseph was a goodly person, and well

favored.
Genesis 39:1-6

Day # 2
Prayer for Obedience

So Samuel said [to Saul]: "Has the Lord as
great delight in burnt offerings and sacrifices,
as in obeying the voice of the Lord? Behold, to
obey is better than sacrifice, and to heed than
the fat of rams."
1 Samuel 15:22

"Author and Pastor Ben Patterson was
mountain climbing with three friends when he
took an ill-advised short-cut and got separated
from the others and found himself trapped on
an icy ledge. When his friends finally found
him, they talked him off the ledge, telling him
where to put his feet (which he couldn't see) as
he inched off the ledge. Only by obeying the
instructions of his more-experienced friends
was he saved from certain death.

There is value in obedience. Often we think we

have a better idea or plan than God. But once we execute our plan we lose the opportunity of seeing how beneficial God's plan would have been. Saul, the first king of Israel, learned the hard way that God delights in obedience more than anything else. When Saul substituted his plan for God's, it cost him the throne of Israel (1 Samuel 15).

One of the greatest challenges of the Christian life is to learn that God says what He says *for a reason.* Better to take Him at His Word" (Source: DavidJeremiah.org/Better to Obey).

Sacrifice and offering thou didst not desire; mine ears hast thou opened: burnt offering and sin offering hast thou not required. Then said I, Lo, I come: in the volume of the book it is written of me, I delight to do thy will, O my God: yea, thy law is within my heart.
Psalm 40:6-8

Obedience - Reasoning = Faith

Day # 3

Prayer to Make Your Body a Temple

Or do you not know that your body is the temple of the Holy Spirit who is in you, whom you have from God, and you are not your own? 1 Corinthians 6:19

"The Solomon's Temple, perhaps the most beautiful building ever constructed, cannot compare with the temple of our bodies. Just one statistic will suffice: If you took all the blood vessels out of your body and laid them in a straight line, they would stretch close to 100,000 miles. We are fearfully and wonderfully made!

On the Day of Pentecost, the Holy Spirit descended on the believers who were meeting together, and tongues of fire sat upon each of them. They were all filled with the Holy Spirit (Acts 2:3-4). That day the Spirit came down from heaven to indwell every believer, and now our very bodies are His temples. He does His work through our hands, feet, minds, and mouths. He lives within us.

Just as we grieve a little when passing a dilapidated church building, so we should grieve when we don't care for our bodies as we should. We have a duty to stay as healthy as possible and glorify God through our body, which is the temple of the Spirit. Your Body, the Temple of God" (Source: Twisted Sister Yoga, LLC./Your Body, A Temple).

Yet a little while, and the world seeth me no more; but ye see me: because I live, ye shall live also. At that day ye shall know that I am in my Father, and ye in me, and I in you.
He that hath my commandments, and keepeth them, he it is that loveth me: and he that loveth me shall be loved of my Father, and I will love him, and will manifest myself to him.
Judas saith unto him, not Iscariot, Lord, how is it that thou wilt manifest thyself unto us, and not unto the world? Jesus answered and said unto him, If a man love me, he will keep my words: and my Father will love him, and we will come unto him, and make our abode with him.
He that loveth me not keepeth not my sayings: and the word which ye hear is not mine, but the

Father's which sent me. These things have I spoken unto you, being yet present with you.
John 14:19-25

During daily prayer encouragements, W. Nee *clarified to the church that Christ wants to sanctify our body and fill it with the Holy Spirit so that it can be a vessel for Him.*

Day # 4
Pray to Become a Man of "Better" Principle

"Look!" [the king] answered, "I see four men loose, walking in the midst of the fire; and they are not hurt, and the form of the fourth is like the Son of God."
Daniel 3:25

"The 'better' principle is illustrated in a number of different ways in Proverbs. For instance, *Proverbs 15:16* says, 'Better is a little with the fear of the Lord, than great treasure with trouble.' And *Proverbs 16:8* reminds us that 'Better is a little with righteousness than vast revenues without justice.'

Another example of the 'better' principle is this: Being in God's will in a difficult place is better than being out of God's will in an easy place. Or, said another way: Being in a hard place *with* God is better than being in an easy place *without* Him. There are examples in Scripture. When the three young Hebrew men found themselves in a fiery furnace in Babylon, they discovered that another person—'like the Son of God'—was with them. And they came out alive. Likewise, when the disciples were crossing the Sea of Galilee with Jesus in a storm, His presence assured their survival.

God may not always keep us out of hard places, but He is always with us. A hard place with Him is better than an easy place without Him" (Source: Full Gospel Businessmen's Training/The Better Principle/W.S. Plumer).

And the same day, when the even was come, he saith unto them, Let us pass over unto the other side. And when they had sent away the multitude, they took him even as he was on the

ship. And there were also with him other little ships. And there arose a great storm of wind, and the waves beat into the ship, so that it was now full. And he was in the hinder part of the ship, asleep on a pillow: and they awake him, and say unto him, Master, carest thou not that we perish? And he arose, and rebuked the wind, and said unto the sea, Peace, be still. And the wind ceased, and there was a great calm. And he said unto them, Why are ye so fearful? how is it that ye have no faith? And they feared exceedingly, and said one to another, What manner of man is this, that even the wind and the sea obey him?
Mark 4:35-41

"The more terrible the storm, the more necessary the anchor." W. S. Plumer

Day # 5
<u>Pray for a Heart of Courage</u>

But if [God doesn't rescue us], let it be known to you, O king, that we do not serve your gods, nor will we worship the gold image which you

have set up.
Daniel 3:18

"In the 1939 film *The Wizard of Oz*, Dorothy's friend the Tin Man desires a heart, and the Cowardly Lion wants courage. So, the Wizard of Oz gives the Tin Man a heart-shaped watch and the Lion a medal proving he has courage. But if the Lion really wanted courage he should have received the Tin Man's heart—since 'courage' comes from the Latin *cor,* the word for 'heart.' Courage is a matter of heart.

In ancient times (and the Bible), 'heart' referred to the seat of emotions, the intellect, or the will. In short, when a person has "heart," he or she has character, commitment, intelligence, and volition. Combine all those and you will find a person with courage. That's what we find in the three young Hebrew men in Babylon *(Daniel 3:18)* and in Joshua as he led the Israelites into Canaan *(Joshua 24:14-15)*.

How do we gain strength of mind, heart, and soul? How do we become a person of courage? By feeding on, and standing on, God's Word in every circumstance" (Source: DavidJeremiah.org).

Now therefore fear the LORD, and serve him in sincerity and in truth: and put away the gods which your fathers served on the other side of the flood, and in Egypt; and serve ye the LORD. And if it seem evil unto you to serve the LORD, choose you this day whom ye will serve; whether the gods which your fathers served that were on the other side of the flood, or the gods of the Amorites, in whose land ye dwell: but as for me and my house, we will serve the LORD. **Joshua 24:14-15**
"I will not flee, much less recant, so may the Lord Jesus strengthen me." Martin Luther

Day # 6
Pray for the Words of Revival to be on Your Tongue

You shall speak My words to them, whether they hear or whether they refuse.
Ezekiel 2:7

"After one hundred years of Protestantism and in the wake of the Thirty Years' War, Philipp Jakob Spener, a German pastor, called people back to regular Bible study, prayer, and piety. The Church had grown cold, and many Christians had become indifferent. Spener exhorted people to trust God completely and to produce good works. He felt pastors should rededicate themselves to ministering the Word of God to their people, and that youth should be well-instructed in Scripture.

For all this, Spener was frequently attacked, yet the revival begun under his ministry—called Pietism—touched Christianity in a way felt to this day.

It seems odd we'd be attacked for calling people back to God, back to Bible study, prayer, faith, and good works. Yet we live in a culture increasingly opposed to spiritual revival. Don't be intimidated. God is able to protect us when we take a stand for Him. We need revival in our lands, and it won't come unless it begins in us" (Source: Full Gospel Businessmen's Training/Philip Spener).

And he said unto me, Son of man, stand upon thy feet, and I will speak unto thee. And the spirit entered into me when he spake unto me, and set me upon my feet, that I heard him that spake unto me. And he said unto me, Son of man, I send thee to the children of Israel, to a rebellious nation that hath rebelled against me: they and their fathers have transgressed against me, even unto this very day.
For they are impudent children and stiffhearted. I do send thee unto them; and thou shalt say unto them, Thus saith the Lord GOD. And they, whether they will hear, or whether they will forbear, (for they are a rebellious house,) yet shall know that there hath been a prophet among them.
And thou, son of man, be not afraid of them, neither be afraid of their words, though briers and thorns be with thee, and thou dost dwell among scorpions: be not afraid of their words, nor be dismayed at their looks, though they be a rebellious house. And thou shalt speak my

words unto them, whether they will hear, or whether they will forbear: for they are most rebellious. But thou, son of man, hear what I say unto thee; Be not thou rebellious like that rebellious house: open thy mouth, and eat that I give thee. And when I looked, behold, an hand was sent unto me; and, lo, a roll of a book was therein; And he spread it before me; and it was written within and without: and there was written therein lamentations, and mourning, and woe.
Ezekiel 2:1-10

"If we succeed in getting the people to seek eagerly and diligently in the book of life for their joy, their spiritual life will be wonderfully strengthened and they will become altogether different people." P. Spener

Day # 7
Pray for Wholesomeness

In all things showing yourself to be a pattern of good works; in doctrine showing integrity, reverence, incorruptibility.

Titus 2:7

"In mathematics two of the basic kinds of numbers are integers and fractions: 2, 100, and 56 are integers, while ½, ¼, and 2.5 are fractions. *Integers*, from a Latin root meaning 'whole' or "entire." The word *integrity* comes from the same root; a person with integrity cannot be divided in beliefs or morality based on varying circumstances.

When the apostle Paul wrote to his young pastoral protégé, Timothy, he told him to show 'integrity' in doctrine, to be incorruptible in belief and in actions. Paul wanted Timothy to hold fast to the truth of God, not allowing himself to be divided. A person of integrity obeys the whole counsel of God every day, in every circumstance. Daniel's three friends in Babylon demonstrated integrity when they were threatened with being burned alive (Daniel 3:16-18). They told the king they would not divide their allegiance, that they would maintain their faith in God and His promises. That is integrity.

Are you a whole person or a fractioned person today? If your beliefs, and therefore your actions, have become divided, gather them back together as you commit to God and His Word" (Source: Turning Point for God/A Whole Person/ David Jeremiah).

But speak thou the things which become sound doctrine: That the aged men be sober, grave, temperate, sound in faith, in charity, in patience. The aged women likewise, that they be in behaviour as becometh holiness, not false accusers, not given to much wine, teachers of good things; That they may teach the young women to be sober, to love their husbands, to love their children, To be discreet, chaste, keepers at home, good, obedient to their own husbands, that the word of God be not blasphemed. Young men likewise exhort to be sober minded. In all things shewing thyself a pattern of good works: in doctrine shewing uncorruptness, gravity, sincerity, Sound speech, that cannot be condemned; that he that is of the contrary part may be ashamed, having no evil thing to say of you.

Exhort servants to be obedient unto their own masters, and to please them well in all things; not answering again; Titus 2:1-9

"Integrity of heart is indispensable." J. Calvin

Day # 8

Pray to Be Ready for the Second Coming of Jesus

He who testifies to these things says, "Surely I am coming quickly." Amen. Even so, come, Lord Jesus!
Revelation 22:20

"Have you seen videos of labor pain simulation? Electric currents to the abdomen of men cause muscle contractions that approximate the pain a woman feels during childbirth. Most childbirths are prolonged and painful. So it's no surprise that Paul used labor pain as a way to illustrate the "groans and labors" that "the whole creation" is experiencing as it waits for the birth of the new earth *(Romans 8:22-25).*

But it's not just "creation" that is groaning and laboring; "we ourselves groan within ourselves, eagerly waiting for . . . the redemption of our body." It is painfully obvious that things are not right with the world. And if we are honest with ourselves, things are not always right with us either. We know the world needs to be fixed, and we long for the day when there will be no more tears, death, sin, or pain *(Revelation 21:4)*.

But Jesus did not tell us when He would return *(Mark 13:32; Acts 1:6-7)*. What to do in the interim? Pray as the apostle John prayed: "Even so, come, Lord Jesus!" *(Revelation 22:20)* And live in a manner that proves our longing for His appearing" *(1 Timothy 6:11-16)*. (Source: Turning Point for God/Labor Pains/Charles Spurgeon)

For we know that the whole creation groaneth and travaileth in pain together until now. And not only they, but ourselves also, which have the firstfruits of the Spirit, even we ourselves groan within ourselves, waiting for the adoption, to wit, the redemption of our body. For we are saved by hope: but hope that is seen is not hope: for what a man seeth, why doth he yet hope for? But if we hope for that we see not, then do we with patience wait for it. Romans 8:22-25

"God's people may groan, but they may not grumble." C. Spurgeon

Day # 9
<u>Pray for God's Will to be Done for Your Destiny</u>

Then [Jesus] looked at them and said, "What then is this that is written: 'The stone which the builders rejected has become the chief cornerstone'?"
Luke 20:17

"In the ancient world, when a new stone building was to be constructed, the first stone set in place was the cornerstone. Great care was taken with the carving of the cornerstone since it determined the direction of the walls that were built out from it. The cornerstone was the most important stone in the building.

To the religious leaders of His day, Jesus intimated that He was the "chief cornerstone." But of what? To what building was Jesus referring when He declared Himself to be the chief cornerstone? He didn't say, but the apostle Paul did in Ephesians 2:19-22. Jesus initiated the building of what is becoming "a holy temple in the Lord"—that is, the Church of all true believers, also called "the household of God." Jesus is the chief cornerstone, "the apostles and prophets" are the foundation, and we are the "living stones" (1 Peter 2:5) God is using to build the temple in which His presence dwells.

Everything depends on Jesus; He is the cornerstone that provides direction and structure to the Church. Our faith begins and ends with Him" (Source: DavidJermiah.org/The Cornerstone/ Matthew Henry).

Now therefore ye are no more strangers and

foreigners, but fellow citizens with the saints, and of the household of God; And are built upon the foundation of the apostles and prophets, Jesus Christ himself being the chief corner stone; In whom all the building fitly framed together groweth unto an holy temple in the Lord: In whom ye also are builded together for an habitation of God through the Spirit.
Ephesians 2:19-22

"Christ is our temple, in whom, by faith, all believers meet." M. Henry

Day # 10
Pray to be Kingdom Minded

And in the days of these kings the God of heaven will set up a kingdom which shall never be destroyed; and the kingdom shall not be left to other people; it shall break in pieces and consume all these kingdoms, and it shall stand forever.
Daniel 2:44

"Besides his scientific expertise, Sir Isaac

Newton (d. 1727) was a historian. He wrote a lengthy book—*The Chronology of Ancient Kingdoms Amended*—that outlined the chronology (rise and fall) of six ancient kingdoms: Greek, Egyptian, Assyrian, Babylonians and Medes, Israelite, and Persian. We could add more kingdoms to the ones Newton wrote about; the pages of history tell of many. There is something in the nature of man that wants to create a kingdom and rule over it—probably a vestige of man's commission to rule over God's kingdom on earth *(Genesis 1:28).* But all such human kingdoms have been temporary. Their failure should serve as a reminder that a permanent, eternal Kingdom is coming—first for a thousand years on earth *(Revelation 20:1-4)*, then on the new earth for eternity *(Revelation 21:1-3).*

Do not be discouraged at man's failed attempts to govern himself. Instead look for the coming of the One whose government will know no end" (Source: DavidJeremiah.org/Kingdoms vs. the Kingdom/Martyn Lloyd Jones).

For unto us a child is born, unto us a son is given: and the government shall be upon his shoulder: and his name shall be called Wonderful, Counsellor, The mighty God, The everlasting Father, The Prince of Peace. Of the increase of his government and peace there shall be no end, upon the throne of David, and upon his kingdom, to order it, and to establish it with judgment and with justice from henceforth even for ever. The zeal of the LORD *of hosts will perform this. Isaiah 9:6-7*

History can be understood only in terms of God's kingdom.
D. M. Lloyd-Jones

Day # 11
Pray for Knowledge of the Future

I am God, and there is none like Me, declaring the end from the beginning.
Isaiah 46:9-10

Last fall Business Insider ran an article on

books that have predicted the future. For example, Gulliver's Travels described a planet with two moons, and 150 years later astronomers noticed Mars had two moons. Twenty Thousand Leagues Under the Sea anticipated the invention of the submarine. H. G. Wells predicted the atomic bomb in his 1914 novel The World Set Free. Martin Caidin's Cyborg envisioned bionic limbs. Science fiction writers use their imagination to create scenarios that may later match reality.

But only one book predicts the future unfailingly, far in advance, and with a proven track record of total accuracy. God's quality of omniscience (He is all-knowing) includes every future contingency and event. And He has revealed those future events for our preparation and anticipation. God has foretold the future because He knows it—and He controls it.

We have hope because God is in control of the future, and His every promise anticipates a fulfillment that will eventually culminate in His glorious return. Our hearts should overflow with gladness" (Source: StopAndPrayTV/Knowing the Future/ J. Dwight Pentecost).

Remember this, and shew yourselves men: bring it again to mind, O ye transgressors. Remember the former things of old: for I am God, and there is none else; I am God, and there is none like me, declaring the end from the beginning, and from ancient times the things that are not yet done, saying, My counsel shall stand, and I will do all my pleasure: Calling a ravenous bird from the east, the man that executeth my counsel from a far country: yea, I have spoken it, I will also bring it to pass; I have purposed it, I will also do it. Hearken unto me, ye stouthearted, that are far from righteousness: I bring near my righteousness; it shall not be far off, and my salvation shall not tarry: and I will place salvation in Zion for Israel my glory. Isaiah 46:8-13

"God, the architect of the ages, has seen fit to take us into His confidence concerning His plan for the future and has revealed His

purpose and program in detail in the Word." J. D. Pentecost

Day # 12
Pray for a "First Response Attitude" of Praise

Then the secret was revealed to Daniel in a night vision. So Daniel blessed the God of heaven.
Daniel 2:19

"Sadly, 'first responders' is a term we know all too well today. They are the trained technicians who are the first on the scene of a tragedy or disaster: police, medical personnel, firefighters, wilderness and water rescuers, various military units, humanitarian teams, and others. What is the first response of the first responders? It is to save, to help, to give aid and comfort wherever needed.

Christians might be considered 'first responders' in the world as well, offering whatever practical help we can to those in need. But what about our 'first response'? Paul gives three good ones in 1 Thessalonians 5:16-18: rejoice, pray, give thanks. Specifically, how often do we couple prayer and thanksgiving together? When we pray, and God answers, what is our first response? In Scripture, it is often praise before anything else. When Daniel and his three friends prayed for God's intervention in Babylon, the answer came and Daniel's first response was to praise God (Daniel 2:17-23).

God is to be praised and thanked in all things, as Paul wrote—but especially when He answers our prayers" (Source: Joseph Addison).

O give thanks unto the LORD, for he is good: for his mercy endureth for ever.
Let the redeemed of the LORD say so, whom he hath redeemed from the hand of the enemy;And gathered them out of the lands, from the east, and from the west, from the north, and from the south.
They wandered in the wilderness in a solitary way; they found no city to dwell in.

Hungry and thirsty, their soul fainted in them.
*Then they cried unto the L*ORD *in their trouble,*
and he delivered them out of their distresses.
And he led them forth by the right way, that
they might go to a city of habitation.
*Oh that men would praise the L*ORD *for his*
goodness, and for his wonderful works to the
children of men!
Psalm 107:1-8

"When all Thy mercies, O my God, my rising
soul surveys, transported with the view, I'm lost
in wonder, love, and praise." J. Addison

Day #13
Pray that the Intercessors Arise

Now it came to pass in those days that [Jesus]
went out to the mountain to pray, and
continued all night in prayer to God.
Luke 6:12

"Officially, church historians recognized seven
ecumenical church councils held between A.D.
325 and A.D. 787. The first, the First Council of

Nicaea, met to agree on the nature of Jesus of Nazareth as both Son of God and Son of Man, as both fully divine and fully human.

The humanity of Christ, while at the same time divine, is hard to understand. But thankfully, Scripture gives us illustrations: Like us, Jesus suffered, experienced hunger, required sleep, ate ood, and had limits on His knowledge (*Mark 13:32*). One of the most striking and helpful illustrations of Jesus' humanity was His prayer life. We might think that, if Jesus was truly divine, He would have had no need to pray for knowledge, guidance, or help. Yet He did, following the example of godly men like Daniel in Babylon *(Daniel 2:16-18)*. Jesus repeatedly said that He only did what the Father showed Him to do *(John 5:19)*, and prayer was His means.

If Jesus, the Son of God, needed to go to His Father in prayer for strengthening and guidance, how much more do we (*Psalm 32:6*)?" (Source: DavidJeremiah.org/The Need for Prayer/ E.M. Bounds)

*Then Daniel went in, and desired of the king
that he would give him time, and that he would
shew the king the interpretation.*
*Then Daniel went to his house, and made the
thing known to Hananiah, Mishael, and
Azariah, his companions: That they would
desire mercies of the God of heaven
concerning this secret; that Daniel and his
fellows should not perish with the rest of the
wise men of Babylon.*
Daniel 2:16-18

Day # 14
Pray for the Desire to Become a Hunter

*He also chose David His servant, and took him
from the sheepfolds...to shepherd Jacob His
people.*
Psalm 78:70-71

"When Jason Cruise was pastoring a church,
he sometimes felt guilty because he wanted to
be hunting. One day it dawned on him God
was calling him to minister to sportsmen. In the
NIV Outdoorsman Bible, he wrote of the

moment, "God's heart connected with mine and pushed me toward the idea that I could use my passion for hunting to bring him glory…. When I was a young boy stomping through the woods, I had no clue that God was preparing me to hunt with a purpose…or that I'd get the honor of speaking to hunters across the nation…and yet do it all in the name of Jesus.

The Lord gives us passions, purposes, and life experiences—like hunting or shepherding—to prepare us for the personal and unique ministry He has for us. No experiences of life are wasted. He prepares us to stand up for Him, and every part of your background can fashion you for what He wants you to do today" (Source: DavidJeremiah.org/I'd Rather be Hunting/Jason Cruise).

Moreover he refused the tabernacle of Joseph, and chose not the tribe of Ephraim:
But chose the tribe of Judah, the mount Zion which he loved. And he built his sanctuary like high palaces, like the earth which he hath

established forever. He chose David also his servant, and took him from the sheepfolds: From following the ewes great with young he brought him to feed Jacob his people, and Israel his inheritance. So he fed them according to the integrity of his heart; and guided them by the skilfulness of his hands. Psalm 78:67-72

"Monumental changes often occur in simple, quiet moments, and it's in those few seconds that a person makes a clean break with an old way of living and never looks back." J. Cruise

Day #15
Pray for the Conspicuous Hand of God Over You

The Lord your God cares. Deuteronomy 11:12

"In a letter to Brigadier General Thomas Nelson, George Washington marveled at how God's hand had protected him and given success to the cause of liberty: 'The hand of

Providence has been so conspicuous in all this, that he must be worse than an infidel that lacks faith, and… has not gratitude enough to acknowledge his obligations'.

In the middle of life's battles, we're tempted to question God's ordering of our circumstances, but every follower of Christ can look back and see the conspicuous hand of God's Providence. He is committed to caring for us, watching over us, and giving us strength when we are within His will.

Moses reminded the Israelites that God was taking them into a land of hills and valleys, of water and streams, 'a land for which the Lord your God cares; the eyes of the Lord your God are always on it, from the beginning of the year to the very end of the year'" *(Deuteronomy 11:11-12) (Source: DavidJeremiah.org/The Conspicuous Hand/W.A. Criswell).*

Humble yourselves therefore under the mighty hand of God, that he may exalt you in due time:Casting all your care upon him; for he

careth for you.
1 Peter 5:6-7

"That's the way He cares for us too—every
day, all year long, always.
[The Lord] loves, and cares, and sympathizes,
and understands, and seeks, and saves, and
forgives, and helps, and encourages, and
walks by our side… taking care of us in life
when we can't take care of ourselves." W. A.
Criswell

Day # 16
<u>Pray to be Committed</u>

For His eyes are on the ways of man, and He
sees all his steps.
Job 34:21

"There's an old folktale about a man who
wanted to sneak into his neighbor's fields to
steal some wheat. He waited for a dark,
moonless night, and he asked his young
daughter to be the lookout. 'Call if anyone sees
me,' he told her. Just as he was stuffing grain

into his apron, the little girl shouted, 'Father, someone sees you!' The man dropped his grain and ran to her in a panic asking, 'Who was it? Who saw me?' She replied, "Someone above is watching you."

Proverbs 15:3 says, "The eyes of the Lord are in every place, keeping watch on the evil and the good." Maintaining our integrity in times of pressure brings glory to God.

"But God isn't the only one watching us. Others see us more clearly than we think, and we can't hide our deceit and infidelity forever. *Proverbs 28:13* says, 'He who covers his sins will not prosper.'

We have to be committed to our commitments, to keeping our word and honoring our pledges. A heart of integrity remains committed to the holy and omniscient God who desires honesty in our hearts" (Source: Full Gospel Businessmen's Training/ Committed to Our Commitments/ John Maxwell).

The just man walketh in his integrity: his children are blessed after him.
A king that sitteth in the throne of judgment scattereth away all evil with his eyes.
Who can say, I have made my heart clean, I am pure from my sin?
Divers weights, and divers measures, both of them are alike abomination to the LORD.
Even a child is known by his doings, whether his work be pure, and whether it be right.
The hearing ear, and the seeing eye, the LORD hath made even both of them.
Proverbs 20:7-12

"Integrity is not so much what we do as much as who we are." J. Maxwell

Day # 17
<u>Pray for Strength During Pressing Times</u>

Tribulation produces perseverance; and perseverance, character; and character, hope.
Romans 5:3-4

"Recently a student was asked to give a talk at

his church, and he spoke of the importance of perseverance, but he didn't know how to correctly pronounce that word. Throughout his talk, he kept talking about *presseverance*. His listeners smiled and nodded in agreement because they fully understood that perseverance really is press-everance. It's the quality of pressing forward whatever comes. We demonstrate our integrity when we stick with our commitments without wavering, even when grueling times arrive. The apostle Paul emphasized this quality over and over. He told the Romans that the quality of perseverance created hopeful hearts (Romans 5:3-4). He told the Corinthians about his own perseverance as he labored among them and faced great opposition (2 Corinthians 12:12). He told the Ephesians to be "watchful to this end with all perseverance and supplication for all the saints" (Ephesians 6:18). And he reminded Timothy, "But you have carefully followed my doctrine, manner of life, purpose, faith, longsuffering, love, perseverance (2 Timothy 3:10).

Let's be true to our commitments to God and others as we "press toward the goal for the prize of the upward call of God in Christ Jesus" (Philippians 3:14) (Source: DavidJeremiah.org/Pressing/J. Sidlow Baxter).

Therefore being justified by faith, we have peace with God through our Lord Jesus Christ: By whom also we have access by faith into this grace wherein we stand, and rejoice in hope of the glory of God. And not only so, but we glory in tribulations also: knowing that tribulation worketh patience; And patience, experience; and experience, hope: And hope maketh not ashamed; because the love of God is shed abroad in our hearts by the Holy Ghost which is given unto us.
Romans 5:1-5

"Whenever God sends a trial with one hand, He gives grace with the other." J. S. Baxter

Day # 18
Pray for Faith in Faithless Times

But the righteous shall live by his faith.
Habakkuk 2:4

"The prophet Habakkuk left us an interesting book. Its three short chapters are essentially a counseling session between Habakkuk and God, for the prophet was troubled by the turbulent times in which he lived. He couldn't understand why his culture had crumbled and why the streets of his city had become so lawless, so godless. He prayed about it in chapter 1; and in chapter 2, God told Habakkuk to trust Him and to live by faith (verse 4), for "the Lord is in His holy temple," and one day "the earth will be filled with the knowledge of the glory of the Lord, as the waters cover the sea (verses 20, 14).

In response Habakkuk composed a hymn of rejoicing in his third and final chapter, saying, "The Lord God is my strength; He will make my feet like deer's feet, and He will make me walk on my high hills" (verse 19).

When the way becomes rough, trust Him who

is still in His holy temple. He will give you hinds' feet on high places" (Source: David Jeremiah/Faith in Faithless Times).
May all bow to the scepter of our Lord, Jesus Christ, and the whole earth be filled with His glory" (Source: Dr. David Jeremiah).

Although the fig tree shall not blossom, neither shall fruit be in the vines; the labor of the olive shall fail, and the fields shall yield no meat; the flock shall be cut off from the fold, and there shall be no herd in the stalls: Yet I will rejoice in the LORD, I will joy in the God of my salvation. The LORD God is my strength, and he will make my feet like hinds' feet, and he will make me to walk upon mine high places. To the chief singer on my stringed instruments.
Habakkuk 3:17-19

Day # 19
Pray and Magnify the Lord

God reigns over the nations; God sits on His holy throne.
Psalm 47:8

"Does today's breaking news frustrate you? Probably. The world's headlines are enough to make our heads spin and our spirits sag. But lay aside the newspaper or turn off the cable news and read Psalm 47 aloud. It will only take 53 seconds at a reasonable speed.

The writer tells us to clap our hands and to shout in triumph (verse 1) for God is awesome, the King of the earth (verse 2). He will subdue peoples and nations (verse 3). We can sing His praises because He reigns over the nations and sits on His throne (verses 6-8). He is greater than all the leaders. He is highly exalted (verse 9).

Jesus came to die and rise again, ushering in His kingdom. We are His kingdom now, but one day His kingdom will fully come. Circumstances are aligning for His return and one day soon the kingdoms of this world will be the kingdoms of our Lord and of His Christ.

Jesus may come in the next 53 seconds. So

let's not lose a minute in anxious fretting about this world. Let's hold tightly to the truth of Psalm 47 and remember Who is truly in charge" (Source: David Jeremiah/53 Seconds/Harry Ironside).

O clap your hands, all ye people; shout unto God with the voice of triumph. For the LORD most high is terrible; he is a great King over all the earth. He shall subdue the people under us, and the nations under our feet. He shall choose our inheritance for us, the excellency of Jacob whom he loved. Selah.
God is gone up with a shout, the LORD with the sound of a trumpet. Sing praises to God, sing praises: sing praises unto our King, sing praises. For God is the King of all the earth: sing ye praises with understanding.
God reigneth over the heathen: God sitteth upon the throne of his holiness. The princes of the people are gathered together, even the people of the God of Abraham: for the shields of the earth belong unto God: he is greatly exalted.
Psalm 47

"When He reigns there will be no one to dispute His Word, for He will be the only Potentate." H. Ironside

Day # 20
<u>Pray to Go All the Way</u>

You shall remember that the Lord your God led you all the way these forty years in the wilderness.
Deuteronomy 8:2

"Sidney Cox was nineteen when he emigrated from England to Canada. It was 1907, and he never saw his parents again. But the next year he found Christ as Savior and soon began serving the Lord. In 1915, he married a Salvation Army coworker, Violet Henderson, and for the rest of their lives Sidney and Violet served the Lord in Canada and the United States. Sidney passed away in 1975 in Birmingham, Alabama, and perhaps you've never known of his name. But it's possible you grew up singing his Sunday school songs like

The Man Who Prays

'Deep and Wide' and 'I Love Him Better Every Day.'

Or this one: 'My Lord knows the way through the wilderness. All I have to do is follow…. Strength for today is mine all the way, and all that I need for tomorrow…. My Lord knows the way through the wilderness. All I have to do is follow.'

Even if you don't know the song, perhaps you know the experience. If you're in the wilderness today, remember your Guide and follow Him all the way" (Source: Full Gospel Businessmen's Training/All the Way/Fanny Crosby).

O give thanks unto the LORD, for he is good: for his mercy endureth forever. Let the redeemed of the LORD say so, whom he hath redeemed from the hand of the enemy; And gathered them out of the lands, from the east, and from the west, from the north, and from the south. They wandered in the wilderness in a solitary way; they found no city to dwell in. Hungry and

thirsty, their soul fainted in them. Then they cried unto the LORD in their trouble, and he delivered them out of their distresses.
And he led them forth by the right way, that they might go to a city of habitation.
Oh that men would praise the LORD for his goodness, and for his wonderful works to the children of men! For he satisfieth the longing soul, and filleth the hungry soul with goodness. Psalm 107:1-9

"All the way my Savior leads me, what have I to ask beside? Can I doubt His tender mercy, who through life has been my Guide?" F. Crosby

Day # 21
Pray to Make the Word of God Your Law

This Book of the Law shall not depart from your mouth, but you shall meditate in it day and night, that you may observe to do according to all that is written in it. For then you will make your way prosperous, and then you will have good success.

Joshua 1:8
"The primary lesson of life with God is not complicated: His Word (His leading and instruction) is given for our blessing and our benefit. God honors those who honor Him and follow His instructions in this life" (Source: Full Gospel Businessman's Training/It's Not Complicated/N.T. Wright).

Blessed are the undefiled in the way, who walk in the law of the LORD. Blessed are they that keep his testimonies, and that seek him with the whole heart. They also do no iniquity: they walk in his ways. Thou hast commanded us to keep thy precepts diligently. O that my ways were directed to keep thy statutes!
Then shall I not be ashamed, when I have respect unto all thy commandments. I will praise thee with uprightness of heart, when I shall have learned thy righteous judgments.
I will keep thy statutes: O forsake me not utterly. Wherewithal shall a young man cleanse his way? by taking heed thereto according to thy word. With my whole heart have I sought thee: O let me not wander from thy

commandments.
Thy word have I hid in mine heart, that I might
not sin against thee. Blessed art thou, O LORD:
teach me thy statutes. With my lips have I
declared all the judgments of thy mouth.
I have rejoiced in the way of thy testimonies, as
much as in all riches. I will meditate in thy
precepts, and have respect unto thy ways.
I will delight myself in thy statutes: I will not
forget thy word.
Psalm 119:1-16

"After the Exodus from Egypt, Israel was in the wilderness on the way to the land God had promised them. But when they approached Canaan, fear overtook them; they failed to believe God's promise of blessing in their new homeland. So that generation spent the next forty years in the wilderness until their children reached adulthood and could enter the land (Numbers 13–14). When that time came, Joshua, their new leader, reminded them of the primary principle of success in walking with God: Follow His Word in all things" (Joshua 1:8) (Source: Full Gospel Businessman's

Training/It's Not Complicated/N.T. Wright).
*"Today, life in this world can seem like a
wilderness, but the principle of success
remains the same: Trust the Lord; obey His
Word; follow His direction in all things:
The Bible is the book of my life. It's the book I
live with, the book I live by, the book I want to
die by." N.T. Wright.*

Day # 22
Pray to Live by God's Grace and Divine Timing

*Every way of a man is right in his own eyes,
but the Lord weighs the hearts.
Proverbs 21:2*

"There is a world invisible to the naked eye
beneath our skin. With every breath we take,
our heart pumps blood through veins and
arteries, minuscule cells reproduce and heal,
and organs perform their functions. If this is
true of the world within the walls of our skin,
how much more is it true of the physical world
surrounding us?

From our perspective it may appear that the unrighteous prosper, while the righteous experience trouble and pain. But when the scales seem incorrectly tipped in this life, remember that God not only created the entire universe, He sees the invisible motives of every heart. He will execute justice. We can trust Him to not only balance the scales of life but to also extend mercy. His plans and purposes are often hidden from us, but God is faithful. Yes, we will face challenging circumstances in life, but we are never alone or out of God's sight. God sees our hidden tears and listens to our whispered prayers—we can trust that when the scales of justice are weighed righteousness will reign" (Source: StopAndPrayTV/Tipping the Scale/Surrounded by God/Max Lucado).

A time to rend, and a time to sew; a time to keep silence, and a time to speak; a time to love, and a time to hate; a time of war, and a time of peace.
Ecclesiastes 3:7-8

"The state of your heart dictates whether you harbor a grudge or give grace, seek self-pity or seek Christ, drink human misery or taste God's mercy." M. Lucado

Day # 23
Pray for God to Mold You

But I did not do so, because of the fear of God. Nehemiah 5:15

"When Nehemiah became governor of the land of Judah, he and his family refused the common practice of having their meals provided from government funds. While there may have been nothing wrong with taxpayer-funded food for the nation's leader, former governors had abused the practice. Their excessive lifestyles had burdened the people, and Nehemiah wanted to avoid even the appearance of wrongdoing. So he paid his own way because he feared God and wanted to protect his integrity for God's sake" (Source: StopAndPrayTV/But I Did Not/David Jeremiah).

He that walketh uprightly walketh surely: but he that perverteth his ways shall be known.
He that winketh with the eye causeth sorrow: but a prating fool shall fall.
The mouth of a righteous man is a well of life: but violence covereth the mouth of the wicked. Hatred stirreth up strifes: but love covereth all sins. In the lips of him that hath understanding wisdom is found: but a rod is for the back of him that is void of understanding.
Wise men lay up knowledge: but the mouth of the foolish is near destruction.
The rich man's wealth is his strong city: the destruction of the poor is their poverty.
The labor of the righteous tendeth to life: the fruit of the wicked to sin. He is in the way of life that keepeth instruction: but he that refuseth reproof erreth.
Proverbs 10:9-17

"Are there areas of your life in which you should draw some lines, erect some barriers, build some fences, and establish some standards? Any habits you should change? Our society has no established moral code, and the standards keep changing. We must not let the world keep rubbing out the lines we draw for ourselves. The Bible calls us to personal holiness, and our integrity comes from the standards we adopt.

Don't let the world around you squeeze you into its own mould, but let God re-mould your minds from within" (Source: StopAndPrayTV/But I Did Not?David Jeremiah).

And be not conformed to this world: but be ye transformed by the renewing of your mind, that ye may prove what is that good, and acceptable, and perfect, will of God.
Romans 12:2

"Everyone with integrity has drawn some lines and said, "Everyone else did these things, but I did not do so." D. Jeremiah

Day # 24
Pray for Unity of the Faith

I, therefore, the prisoner of the Lord, beseech
you to walk worthy of the calling with which you
were called . . . endeavoring to keep the unity
of the Spirit in the bond of peace.
Ephesians 4:1, 3

"*Shema Israel*—'Hear, [O] Israel'—are the first
two words in the Hebrew prayer known as "the
Shema." They are found in Deuteronomy 6:4:
"Hear, O Israel: The Lord our God, the Lord is
one!" The prayer was central to the Jewish
faith as the nation entered Canaan, a land filled
with multitudes of 'gods' The Shema affirmed
that the God of Israel was one God, not many.
To violate that belief was to violate the integrity
of the Jewish faith" (Source:
DavidJeremiah.org/Hear O, Israel/Richard
Baxter).

Put on therefore, as the elect of God, holy and
beloved, bowels of mercies, kindness,
humbleness of mind, meekness, longsuffering;
Forbearing one another, and forgiving one
another, if any man has a quarrel against any:
even as Christ forgave you, so also do ye.

And above all these things put on charity,
which is the bond of perfectness.
Colossians 3:12-14

"The apostle Paul echoed the Shema in his call to Christian unity: "There is one body and one Spirit . . . one hope . . . one Lord, one faith, one baptism; one God and Father of all" (Ephesians 4:4-6). To disrupt the unity of the Body of Christ with dissension or anger is to violate the integrity of God: Father, Son, and Spirit. Because God is one, His people must be one in "the unity of the Spirit in the bond of peace" (Source: DavidJeremiah.org/Hear O, Israel/Richard Baxter).

Endeavouring to keep the unity of the Spirit in
the bond of peace.
Ephesians 4:3

Day # 25
Pray for the Woman in your Life

Forsake foolishness and live, and go in the
way of understanding.

Proverbs 9:6
"In Proverbs 9, we find a woman working hard
to prepare a banquet. She starts by building a
house for it, hewing out seven pillars. Then she
selects the menu, prepares the feast, and
sends maidens who find the highest spots in
town to shout the invitations: 'Come, eat of my
bread and drink of the wine I have mixed'
(verse 5). The woman's name is Wisdom, and
Proverbs 9 describes all the blessings that
come from her menu.

But the chapter ends with another woman: 'A
foolish woman is clamorous; she is simple, and
knows nothing' (verse 13). Lady Folly also
sends invitations into the streets, saying,
'Whoever is simple, let him turn in here' (verse
16). Her meal is junk food that ruins the heart.

Every person on earth goes to one house or
the other for their understanding of life. One or
the other of these addresses is downloaded
onto the GPS of your soul. You'll have a better
life by going to Wisdom's address. There you
can feast on the richness of God's Word, drink

the wine of His thoughts, and be sustained by the energy of His Spirit" (Source: David Jeremiah/The Woman in Your Life/John Piper). *Wisdom hath builded her house, she hath hewn out her seven pillars: She hath killed her beasts; she hath mingled her wine; she hath also furnished her table. She hath sent forth her maidens: she crieth upon the highest places of the city, Whoso is simple, let him turn in hither: as for him that wanteth understanding, she saith to him, Come, eat of my bread, and drink of the wine which I have mingled. Forsake the foolish, and live; and go in the way of understanding. He that reproveth a scorner getteth to himself shame: and he that rebuketh a wicked man getteth himself a blot. Reprove not a scorner, lest he hate thee: rebuke a wise man, and he will love thee. Give instruction to a wise man, and he will be yet wiser: teach a just man, and he will increase in learning. The fear of the LORD is the beginning of wisdom: and the knowledge of the holy is understanding. For by me thy days shall be multiplied, and the years of thy life shall be increased. If thou be wise, thou shalt be wise for thyself: but if thou scornest, thou alone shalt bear it (Proverbs 9:1-12).*

"The scriptures are radiant with divine wisdom. This wisdom shines with the glory of God." J. Piper

Day # 26
Prayer Over Your Priorities

But seek first the kingdom of God and His righteousness, and all these things shall be added to you.
Matthew 6:33

"Do you remember your grammar lessons? In English, two types of adjectives are comparative and superlative. Comparative adjectives rank two different nouns: 'Jim is the taller of the two boys.' Superlative adjectives compare a noun to a group at either the upper end or lower end, 'Jim is the tallest of all' or 'Tom is the smallest of all.' Akin to these rankings are a set of three adjectives that are more subjective: good, better, and best.

In life we would like everything to be clear-cut, making choices easy: good or bad, black or white, yes or no. In reality, most of life—including the Christian life—is more subjective. Among all the options, how do we know if what we do with our time, talent, and treasure is good, better, or best? How do we set priorities for our life? Today, the first day of 2019, is a good day to seek wisdom to make the best choices possible through prayer, Scripture, and wise counsel" (Source: StopAndPrayTV/Choose the Best/J.A. Motyer).

The days of our years are threescore years and ten; and if by reason of strength they be fourscore years, yet is their strength labor and sorrow; for it is soon cut off, and we fly away. Who knoweth the power of thine anger? even according to thy fear, so is thy wrath.
So teach us to number our days, that we may apply our hearts unto wisdom.
Psalm 90:10-12

"Jesus said the best choice is always to make

God's Kingdom our priority, our best choice.
Everything else will fall into place accordingly"
(Source: StopAndPrayTV/Choose the Best/J.A.
Motyer).

"We live by demands when we should live by priorities." J. A. Motyer

Day # 27
Pray for a Desire to Share God's Love

Time is short.
1 Corinthians 7:29

"Two Washington, D.C., residents quit their
jobs to bicycle around the world. Jay Austin
and Lauren Geoghegan described their
adventures on their blog, 'Simply Cycling,'
explaining, 'Because life is short and the world
is big…we want to make the most out of our
youth and good health before they're gone.'
Tragically they were killed by ISIS terrorists
while bicycling in Tajikistan. They were 29.

We know time is short, but we don't always

know how short it is. The writer of Psalm 89:47 says, 'Remember how short my time is.' For those who know Jesus as Savior, our lifespans are as long as eternity; Jesus has given us eternal life. But we have a brief allocation of time on earth, and we don't have a certain promise of even another day.

Let's make the most of the moments God gives us. Don't fritter your time away with endless diversions and distractions. Live purposefully, making the most of the opportunities because the days are evil (Ephesians 5:16). There's a new year coming soon. Let's take advantage of every moment and every day for Christ and His Kingdom" (Source: StopAndPrayTV/Every Moment, Everyday/William J. Reynolds).

See then that ye walk circumspectly, not as fools, but as wise, Redeeming the time, because the days are evil. Wherefore be ye not unwise, but understanding what the will of the Lord is. And be not drunk with wine, wherein is excess; but be filled with the Spirit; Speaking to yourselves in psalms and hymns and spiritual

*songs, singing and making melody in your
heart to the Lord; Giving thanks always for all
things unto God and the Father in the name of
our Lord Jesus Christ;
Submitting yourselves one to another in the
fear of God.
Ephesians 5:15-21*

*"Share His love by sharing of your faith, and
show the world that Jesus Christ is real to you,
every moment and every day." William J.
Reynolds*

Day # 28
Pray for Hopes and Against Fears

*Grant us that we… might serve Him without
fear, in holiness and righteousness before Him
all the days of our life.* Luke 1:74-75
"When Phillips Brooks wrote the carol, 'O Little
Town of Bethlehem,' he coined a phrase that
sums up our emotions about Christmas: 'The
hopes and fears of all the years are met in thee
tonight.' It's too beautiful a line to alter, but let's
remember that the hope of Jesus overcame

the fears of all the years. Because of Jesus we can release our fears, anxieties, apprehensions, and nervous sorrows.

When you read through Luke's Gospel, beginning with the Nativity, you keep running into the phrase, "Do not be afraid." The angel said that to Zacharias in Luke 1:13, to Mary in Luke 1:30, and to the shepherds in Luke 2:10. Jesus later told Simon Peter in Luke 5:10: 'Do not be afraid.' And He told a worried father named Jairus, 'Do not be afraid; only believe (Luke 8:50)" (StopAndPrayTV/The Hopes and Fears/W.J. Reynolds).

And his father Zacharias was filled with the Holy Ghost, and prophesied, saying, Blessed be the Lord God of Israel; for he hath visited and redeemed his people, And hath raised up an horn of salvation for us in the house of his servant David; As he spake by the mouth of his holy prophets, which have been since the world began: That we should be saved from our enemies, and from the hand of all that hate us; To perform the mercy promised to our fathers, and to remember his holy covenant; The oath which he sware to our father Abraham, That he would grant unto us, that we being delivered out of the hand of our enemies might serve him without fear, In holiness and righteousness before him, all the days of our life. And thou, child, shalt be called the prophet of the Highest: for thou shalt go before the face of the Lord to prepare his ways; To give knowledge of salvation unto his people by the remission of their sins,

Through the tender mercy of our God; whereby the dayspring from on high hath visited us,

To give light to them that sit in darkness and in the shadow of death, to guide our feet into the way of peace. And the child grew, and waxed strong in spirit, and was in the deserts till the day of his shewing unto Israel.

Luke 1:67-80

"One of the most powerful prayers is found in Luke 1:76-79, when Zacharias prayed that God would enable us to serve Him without fear all the days of our lives. Whatever is bothering you today, don't be afraid. Serve the Lord

*without fear, in holiness and righteousness, all
the days of your life." W. J. Reynolds.*

Day # 29
Pray for Resistance against Fear

*Then the angel said to [the shepherds], "Do not
be afraid, for behold, I bring you good tidings of
great joy which will be to all people."* Luke 2:10

"Christmas can be the hardest time of the year.
In fact, some people fear the Christmas
season. Perhaps it's the first Christmas after
the death of a loved one. Maybe there are
financial pressures made worse by Christmas
bills. If you are single and without friends or
family nearby, Christmas can be a lonely time.

"There was fear at the very first Christmas.
Zacharias and Elizabeth feared never having a
child (Luke 1:13). Mary feared the future and
becoming a new bride (Luke 1:30). And the
shepherds in the Bethlehem field feared an
encounter with the supernatural (Luke 2:10).
The Christmas message to them is the same

message to us: "Fear not. This is a season of good news and great joy! A Savior has been born who is Christ, the Lord of all." There is no fearful circumstance that cannot be defused by the reality of the Christmas presence of Christ and His Spirit" (Source: David Jeremiah/The Turning Point/Fear Not!)

The fear of the LORD is the beginning of wisdom: and the knowledge of the holy is understanding.
Proverbs 9:10

"Whatever your circumstances today, let the joy be your strength. Trust and know that the God of all grace is your God." D. Jeremiah

Day # 30
Pray for the Desire to Meditate

Your word I have hidden in my heart, that I might not sin against You.
Psalm 119:11

"There are around one thousand quotes,

references, and allusions to the Old Testament in the New Testament. When New Testament writers wrote their Gospels and letters, they might have had Old Testament scrolls with which to check their quotations and references. But what about when Jesus and the apostles quoted the Old Testament 'on the fly'—during the course of their ministry? In those cases they were quoting from memory, not from a scroll. They took the Old Covenant admonition seriously to know God's Word by heart.

Such was the case when Jesus responded to Satan's three temptations in the wilderness— He quoted three verses from Deuteronomy from memory (Matthew 4:1-11). If we are going to defeat Satan's lies and temptations with the truth of God, we must store up the Word of God in our heart like the psalmist—'that [we] might not sin against [God].'

While in the midst of temptation is not the time to begin your search for Scriptures. Begin today to be prepared—to commit God's Word to memory" (Source: Meditate and

Memorize/David Jeremiah/J. Owen).

Blessed is the man that walketh not in the counsel of the ungodly, nor standeth in the way of sinners, nor sitteth in the seat of the scornful. But his delight is in the law of the LORD; *and in his law doth he meditate day and night. And he shall be like a tree planted by the rivers of water, that bringeth forth his fruit in his season; his leaf also shall not wither; and whatsoever he doeth shall prosper.*
Psalm 1:1-3

"Meditate on the word in the Word." *J. Owen*